OXFORD PROGRESSIVE ENGLISH READERS

General Editor: D. H. Howe

Lady Precious Stream

Lady
Precious
Stream

By
S. I. HSIUNG

Retold by
L. W. TAYLOR

HONG KONG

OXFORD UNIVERSITY PRESS

KUALA LUMPUR SINGAPORE TOKYO

Oxford University Press

OXFORD LONDON GLASGOW NEW YORK
TORONTO MELBOURNE WELLINGTON CAPE TOWN
IBADAN NAIROBI DAR ES SALAAM LUSAKA ADDIS ABABA
KUALA LUMPUR SINGAPORE JAKARTA HONG KONG TOKYO
DELHI BOMBAY CALCUTTA MADRAS KARACHI

© *Oxford University Press 1971*
Fifth impression 1976

ISBN 0 19 638235 1

Retold by L.W. Taylor. Illustrated by Andrew Cheng. Simplified according to the language grading scheme especially compiled by D.H. Howe

Printed by Wing Tai Cheung Printing Co. Ltd., 1 Sai On Lane, Hong Kong
Published by Oxford University Press, News Building, North Point, Hong Kong

Contents

PRINCIPAL CHARACTERS OF THE PLAY IN ORDER OF THEIR APPEARANCE

HIS EXCELLENCY WANG YUN, the Prime Minister
MADAM WANG OF THE CHEN FAMILY, his wife
SU, the Dragon General, their eldest son-in-law
WEI, the Tiger General, their second son-in-law
GOLDEN STREAM, their eldest daughter, Su's wife
SILVER STREAM, their second daughter, Wei's wife
PRECIOUS STREAM, their third daughter
HSIEH PING-KUEI, their gardener
HER ROYAL HIGHNESS, THE PRINCESS OF THE WESTERN REGIONS

NOTE ON LANGUAGE

Stage directions 'right' and 'left' refer to the right and left of the stage when you are facing the audience. 'Up' means the back of the stage; 'down' means the front of the stage.

In addition to footnotes, a note on *Language* is provided at the end of the book.

Introduction

A stage performance in China is long. It begins at six or seven in the evening and ends about midnight. But it is made up of eight or nine acts from an equal number of different plays. As no curtain is used, a Western visitor may think that the acting is one continuous play.

The second act of the play *Lady Precious Stream* has moved thousands to tears and the third and fourth have delighted millions. These acts were, as a rule, performed separately and rarely produced as a whole play.

The usual Chinese stage is not at all true to life. It has little scenery and the property man is always present. He usually wears his everyday clothes and walks about among the players. No stage director* or prompter* is needed. This is perhaps simply because the property man is sure to place the chair correctly when the actor ought to sit down, and to provide a cushion when he or she ought to kneel. In the case when a hero* is to die, he can fall down safely, for the property man is always ready and will catch him when he falls.

These actions would certainly not be accepted by a Western audience, but the Chinese accept them or, rather, pretend not to see them. There is, at least, this advantage: if some accident happens to the player or property, the property man can come forward and put it right before the audience can decide whether it is part of the play or not. On a Western stage this would be impossible!

In this play I have not attempted to alter anything. The following pages present a typical play, exactly as produced on a Chinese stage.

London, March 1934   S.I. Hsiung

director,   the person who tells the actors how to act.
prompter,   the person who tells the actors what to say if
            they forget their words.
hero,   the chief man in a play.

Oxford Progressive English Readers Language Scheme

The OPER language grading scheme was especially compiled by D. H. Howe as a guide to the preparation of language teaching material for school pupils and adults learning English as a second or foreign language. The scheme provides lists of words and language structures subdivided into three grades of difficulty and meant to be used in conjunction with each other.

The items were chosen according to two main principles: first, that they are likely to have been learnt or at least encountered *before* the stage indicated; second, that they are frequently occurring and useful, necessary to express a wide range of ideas, and difficult to replace with simpler words or constructions.

Use of the scheme is intended to eliminate unnecessary difficulties of language which would otherwise hinder understanding and enjoyment.

Act I

The empty stage is the garden of Wang Yun, the Prime Minister.
A long stick with some branches and leaves tied to it is fastened to
a chair to act as trees. It is placed on the right by a Property Man
in black. A strange-looking table (to act as rocks) is placed on the
left by another Property Man. These two men stand at the back but   5
we imagine the stage to be empty.

   Two Attendants enter from the right and move to the front of
the stage. They stand facing each other. They are dressed in
flowery gowns.* Wang, the Prime Minister, appears. He has a
very long beard but His Excellency is only a middle-aged man.   10
He has always found life easy and happy but he is sometimes angry
for no reason at all. Although he is very strict in his home, he
finds that it is easier to rule a nation than to rule a family.

   He is dressed in a beautiful embroidered* red gown and a black
head-dress. He walks proudly to the middle of the stage to show   15
that he is the master of the house. One of the two Property Men
comes forward and places a chair, with a pile of cushions on it, be-
hind the Prime Minister.

WANG: I am your humble servant, Wang Yun, the Prime
Minister of the Emperor's court. My wife's name is Chen. Al-   20
though we have been happily married for twenty years we are
still childless. It is true that we have three daughters, but they
are not important. As you know, daughters leave their parents
and become other people's property. My eldest daughter, who is
called Golden Stream, married Su, the Dragon General; the se-   25
cond is called Silver Stream. She married Wei, the Tiger General.
The one I love most is Precious Stream, the youngest. She will be

---

**gown,*   long, loose, flowing coat, usually tied round the
           waist with a belt.
**embroidered,*   sewn with beautiful designs.

sixteen next February. I have decided to choose a husband for her among the rich and young lords, but she refuses to obey my wishes. However, today is New Year's Day. I will spread a feast here in my garden and tell all my family to be present. My wife,
5   my two sons-in-law and my two elder daughters will try to persuade her to obey me. *(He calls.)* Attendants!

ATTENDANTS: Yes, Your Excellency!

WANG: Request Madam to come here.

ATTENDANTS: Yes, Your Excellency.

10   *(One Attendant calls to the right.)*

His Excellency requests the presence of Madam.

A VOICE *(off stage):*   Yes, I will come.

(Two Maids* come in and move to the front of the stage. Madam Wang then enters from the right. She is wearing a dark blue silk
15   *gown with a red skirt, and walks slowly to the middle of the stage.)*

MADAM: I am Chen, the wife of the Prime Minister. I was told that my husband wanted me. *(She turns round.)* My respects to Your Excellency.

WANG: Thank you. My respects to you too. Please sit down.

20   *(Another seat is brought by the Property Man.)*

MADAM *(sitting down):*   May I know why you have asked me to come to the garden?

WANG: Today is New Year's Day, so let us enjoy ourselves. I think it is going to snow. I suggest that we have a feast here in
25   the garden to enjoy the snow. And during the feast I hope you will talk to Precious Stream. Persuade her to marry one of the young lords whom I have approved.

MADAM: I will do as you say but I am afraid it will be useless. She wants to choose her own husband.

30   WANG: Nonsense! A young girl never chooses a husband herself. What about the teachings of Confucius* and Mencius?*

*maid,   female servant.
*Confucius,   he lived from 551 to 478 B.C. and was one of the great religious leaders of the Chinese people. His writings and his teachings have been handed down by his followers and have had, and still have, a great influence.
*Mencius,   was a follower of Confucius.

Young people study them but never follow them. *(He is becoming angry.)*

MADAM: She says that 'Not to force upon others your own opinions' is one of the important teachings of Confucius. She hopes that you will not forget it!   5

WANG: *(blowing into his long beard in anger):*   You have spoiled her. You must not encourage her to disobey me. *(He turns aside and calls.)* Attendants!

ATTENDANTS: Yes, Your Excellency!

WANG: Tell General Su, General Wei, and the ladies to come   10
to see me.

ATTENDANTS: Yes, Your Excellency.

(One of them calls to the right.) His Excellency asks General Su and General Wei and his three daughters to go to see him!

VOICES *(off stage):*   Yes, we are coming!   15

(Enter Su, the Dragon General, and Wei, the Tiger General. They have strange make-up and wear embroidered armour covered with silk gowns. Su, the Dragon General, is a famous soldier. He always wins a battle when he knows more about war than the enemy's general. Yet he never boasts of his victories because he   20 knows that he is not the cleverest general in the land. Wei, the Tiger General, is also a famous soldier. He is a very bad general but he always has very good luck. He knows nothing and is very lazy but he talks a lot. Both Su and Wei march to the front and, standing side by side, face the audience.)   25

SU: Your humble servant, Su, the Dragon General.

WEI: I am Wei, the Tiger General.

(They face each other.)

SU: My dear relative, Wei, you first, please.

WEI: My dear relative, Su, after you, of course.   30

SU: Thank you. Just a moment ago our father-in-law, the Prime Minister, asked us to come to the garden to see him. Do you know why?

WEI: No, I don't. Let us go up and find out.

(Wei goes up first and they stand side by side, facing His Ex-   35 cellency and Madam.)

SU and WEI: Your sons-in-law beg to pay their respects to you.

WANG: Don't stand on ceremony. Please sit down.

SU and WEI: Thank you. *(They sit at their father-in-law's* 5 *side in the chairs provided by the Property Men.)*

(Two young ladies come forward. They are dressed in richly embroidered silk gowns with beautiful skirts. Golden Stream, the eldest daughter of the Wang family, is kind, full of dignity and silent. Silver Stream, the second daughter, is the opposite. She is 10 *gay, talkative, and quick-tempered. She is more like her father than her mother. With delicate steps they move to the front and introduce themselves to the audience.)*

GOLDEN STREAM: Your humble maid, Golden Stream, the eldest daughter of the Wang family. My husband is Su, the 15 Dragon General.

SILVER STREAM: I am Silver Stream, the second daughter of the Wang family. My husband is Wei, the Tiger General, and the most handsome man in the kingdom. *(She looks over her shoulder, to the right and to the left.)* The whole family has been 20 called here and I think I know why. *(She addresses her sister.)* My eldest sister!

GOLDEN STREAM: Yes, my younger sister.

SILVER STREAM: Do you know why Father has called us to come here?

25   GOLDEN STREAM: No, I don't know.

SILVER STREAM *(talking quickly):*   Because of our youngest sister! *(She stretches out three fingers.)* I am sure it is about her. She is not very young now and she is choosing a husband for herself. No wonder! I would do the same if I were in *her* place. 30 But father also wants to choose one for her, and no wonder! I would do the same too if I were in *his* place. And mother...

GOLDEN STREAM *(interrupting her):*   All right. Don't talk so much. Let us go in.

(They go in and bow to their parents.)

35   GOLDEN STREAM and SILVER STREAM: Your daughters have come to pay their respects to you, dear Father and Mother.

WANG: Don't stand on ceremony. Sit down.

GOLDEN STREAM and SILVER STREAM: Thank you. *(Two chairs are placed for them and they sit by their mother's side.)*

SILVER STREAM *(quickly):*   Did you call us here to discuss our youngest sister, Precious Stream?   5

WANG: Eh, yes; no, not really. Today is New Year's Day and we should enjoy ourselves. I think it is going to snow. Let us have a feast here in the garden to enjoy the snow. And during the feast, well...

SILVER STREAM: Oh, I know! And during the feast we will try   10
to persuade Precious Stream to marry one of the young lords whom you have chosen. Am I right?

WANG: Yes, that is exactly what I wish you to do.

GOLDEN STREAM: But if she has someone of her own choice...

WANG: Nonsense, I won't allow it!   15

GOLDEN STREAM: Is that fair, dear Father?

MADAM: Yes, is that fair, dear?

WANG: Well, it is a daughter's duty to obey.

SILVER STREAM *(coming to the rescue):*   Father knows all the important people. Our youngest sister should choose someone   20
he knows. When I was young, Father chose for me too. That was how I married the most handsome man in the kingdom!

WEI: Oh, thank you! *(He covers his face with his sleeve.)*

SILVER STREAM: Keep quiet, please! She is coming.

(Precious Stream, the youngest and the most beautiful daugh-   25
ter of the family, appears from the right with a Maid. She is well-dressed and walks gracefully. She seems to have both her father's and her mother's qualities as well as some of her own charms.)

PRECIOUS STREAM *(to the audience):*   I am your humble maid, Precious Stream, the third and youngest daughter of the   30
Wang family. *(She speaks to the Maid.)* Will you lead me to the garden?

MAID: Yes, my lady.

(They arrive, after walking once round the stage.)

PRECIOUS STREAM: Your daughter pays her respects to you,   35
dear Father and Mother.

WANG: Don't stand on ceremony. Sit down.

PRECIOUS STREAM: Thank you. And my good wishes to my brothers-in-law and my dear sisters.

THEY ALL: We thank you and wish you the same.

5   PRECIOUS STREAM *(sitting beside her sisters)*: May I know why you have called me here, Father?

WANG: Yes. Ahem! Well—the fact is, eh—today—eh— today is—eh—

SILVER STREAM *(quickly)*: Today is New Year's Day. Father
10 wants to enjoy the occasion. It looks as if it is going to snow. Father suggests we should have a feast here in the garden to en- joy the snow. And during the feast he wishes...

WANG *(uneasily)*: Ahem! That is enough, thank you!

PRECIOUS STREAM: Wonderful! Call the servants to arrange
15 the table at once. And while the snow is falling we can ask the gentlemen to write poems for the occasion. I think my brothers- in-law will like that.

SU: Oh, I am not a poet.

WEI: Please don't spoil the fun by asking me to do that.

20 SILVER STREAM: Oh, please don't!

WANG: Attendants, move that big rock to the centre. *(He points to the strange-looking table on the left.)* We want to use it as our table.

ATTENDANTS: Yes, Your Excellency!
25 *(They go to the table and try to move it, but cannot.)* Your Excellency, the rock cannot be moved.

WANG: Nonsense! You are useless!

MADAM: But, my dear, it is too heavy.

WEI: Cowards! If it refuses to be moved, why don't you
30 kick it?

SILVER STREAM: Yes, why don't you kick it?

PRECIOUS STREAM: Dear Father, I really think it is too heavy for them. Why don't you ask my brothers-in-law to move it! They are both famous for their strength.

35   WEI *(aside to Su)*: I think there is going to be trouble. Just leave everything to me.

SU: All right, carry on.

WEI *(to his father-in-law)*:   As our great Confucius said, 'To kill a little chicken, why use a big knife which is made for killing horses?'

WANG *(correcting him)*:   '...for killing oxen' is the ancient saying.

WEI *(quickly)*:   Oh, yes, 'To kill a little chicken, why use a big knife for killing oxen?' as Confucius said. So why should I lift this little rock? If there is a big rock, ten times as large as that, or even larger, then I will easily and gladly lift it.

SILVER STREAM: Yes, I am sure you will.

PRECIOUS STREAM: But if we must kill a chicken and there is no small knife, don't you think that we must use a big knife?

WEI: Well... *(Looking at his wife for help.)*

SILVER STREAM *(who doesn't know what to say)*:   Well!

PRECIOUS STREAM *(smiling)*:   Well!

SU *(a more truthful and practical man)*:   As none of us can move that rock, may I make a suggestion? *(All agree.)* You know the gardener, Hsieh Ping-Kuei. Before working for us he was a street acrobat*...

WEI: That means, a beggar.

SILVER STREAM: Yes, a beggar.

PRECIOUS STREAM: A beggar is a man of words and no deeds; an acrobat is a man of deeds and not of words.

SU *(continuing his suggestion)*:   I once saw him lifting huge stones.

WEI: Yes, I saw him lifting up a stone many times as big as that one. Order him to move it for us.

SILVER STREAM: Yes, order him to do it!

PRECIOUS STREAM: Don't you think this rock is too small for him?

(Wei looks away.)

WANG: Attendants!

ATTENDANTS: Yes, Your Excellency!

WANG: Order the gardener, Hsieh Ping-Kuei, to come here at once.

ATTENDANTS: Yes, Your Excellency!

*acrobat, a person who can do clever tricks with his body.

(One Attendant calls off, left.)

His Excellency orders the gardener, Hsieh Ping-Kuei, to come here at once!

A VOICE *(off stage):*   His Excellency's orders will be obeyed!
(Hsieh Ping-Kuei enters left. He is plainly dressed and is a handsome man. His firm step shows that people can depend on him, and the open book in his hand shows that he has read a lot. He comes forward and bows to the audience.)

HSIEH: I am your humble servant, Hsieh Ping-Kuei. Once I was a beggar, and now I am the gardener to His Excellency the Prime Minister, Wang. There is very little work to be done here, so I am always reading. You see, I wasted my time when I was young. Now I am trying to read and learn as much as I can. *(He shows us the book he was reading.)* I hear that His Excellency is calling me. I will go in and see what he wants. *(He puts the book down his back, turns round, and kneels before Wang.)* Your humble gardener, Hsieh Ping-Kuei. What is Your Excellency's order?

WANG: I want you to move that rock to the centre.

MADAM: We want to use it as a table.

HSIEH: Very well, Your Excellency! *(He gets up and raises the rock over his head, walks round the stage three times, and puts it down in the centre. The others are looking at him with disbelief.)* Is that all right, Your Excellency?

WANG: All right. You can go now.

PRECIOUS STREAM: All of us, and especially General Wei, thank you very much! *(Hsieh bows.)* You may go now.

HSIEH: Thank you, my lady. *(He bows again and goes.)*

WEI: That was simple. I can easily move a rock ten times larger!

WANG: Attendants!

ATTENDANTS: Yes, Your Excellency!

WANG: Serve the feast here.

ATTENDANTS: Yes, Your Excellency!

(An Attendant takes a tray with a wine-pot and some cups on it and puts them one by one on the table. They all rise; their chairs are moved to the three sides of the table and the front is left empty.)

WANG: Precious Stream, my dear daughter, serve the wine.
(Precious Stream serves the wine.) Madam, my honourable sons-
in-law, my dear daughters, please drink.

(They all put their cups to their mouths with their right hand,
and cover them with the sleeves of their left hand. The men throw   5
their heads backwards to show that they empty their cups; the
ladies only drink slowly, a little bit at a time.)

WANG: The wine is excellent. Let us have more.

(Precious Stream serves again, and the same thing is repeated. In the meantime, two chairs are brought forward and placed right and left. Then two old men with long beards enter from the right and left. They each have a black flag rolled up in their right hand. They are helped to stand on chairs and then they unroll their flags. Small white pieces of paper fall from them. Having done this, they come down from the chairs and leave. The chairs are then removed.)

WANG: What a beautiful scene the snow makes! We have wine and snow, let us also have some poems. Who is going to write them? *(He looks at his sons-in-law.)*

SU: I am bad at writing poems. Please excuse me.

GOLDEN STREAM: Father will of course excuse you.

WEI: Everyone knows that I can write poems very well but I cannot write any now because there is no pen and no paper. And it would be cruel to send anyone to get them in this snow. So I will write some poems at home tonight and present them to you tomorrow.

SILVER STREAM: Yes, tomorrow.

WANG *(well pleased):* Yes, very good!

PRECIOUS STREAM: I have brought pen and paper with me, so you can write the poems now. *(She turns to her Maid.)* My maid, hand them to General Wei.

MAID *(taking them out from her long sleeves):* Yes, my lady. *(To Wei.)* Here you are, great General!

(She puts them on the table before Wei.)

WEI: Ah! Thank you! *(Wondering what to do next.)* I am sorry to say that I do not feel like writing any poems now. I remember some poet said: 'To write good poems, one needs perspiration!'* It is cold now, you see. We can't expect any perspiration until summer comes.

WANG: Perspiration? You mean inspiration!*

WEI: Oh, yes! Inspiration! *(He wipes his forehead with his sleeves.)* Not perspiration! Of course, not perspiration.

SILVER STREAM: I know you don't mean perspiration.

*perspiration, sweat.
*inspiration, here means a good idea coming to the mind.

PRECIOUS STREAM: If it is only perspiration that you need, then you must be the greatest poet we have!

WEI *(thinking she is praising him):*   Oh, thank you!

SILVER STREAM: Shame on you. How can you laugh at my husband like this!   5

SU: May I make another suggestion? I once heard the gardener, Hsieh Ping-Kuei, singing beautiful songs in the street. I was told that he composed the songs.

GOLDEN STREAM: Yes, I remember too.

WEI: No, I don't think he composed them.   10

WANG: Yes, he did. I gave him the job as my gardener because he was so clever.

WEI *(relieved):*   Truly, you are the most just Prime Minister in history! Now let him repay some of your kindness by entertaining us with his songs.   15

SILVER STREAM: Yes, if he really can.

WANG: Attendants!

ATTENDANTS: Yes, Your Excellency!

WANG: Order the gardener, Hsieh Ping-Kuei, to come here again.   20

ATTENDANTS: Yes, Your Excellency!

(An Attendant calls to Hsieh and tells him to come. In a moment he is kneeling before Wang, waiting for orders.)

WANG: As we are drinking wine and enjoying the snow, we would like to hear a little poem. I have heard that you are a poet.   25
Give us one of your poems.

MADAM: Yes, give us one.

HSIEH: Your Excellency, I am only one of your workers and my duty to Your Excellency is simply to work.

WEI: Hurrah! Bravo! I said he couldn't!   30

SILVER STREAM: So did I.

SU: Wait a moment. What do you mean, Hsieh Ping-Kuei?

HSIEH: If you want me to write a poem, you must treat me as a gentleman; and I must be invited, not ordered.

WEI: Impossible!   35

SILVER STREAM: The man ought to be whipped.

PRECIOUS STREAM: Why? He is right. A real poet should not

be treated as a workman. Why shouldn't we treat him with pro-
per respect?

WANG: Well, to show that I am a just man I will give you a
seat in that corner, and request you to write a short poem of
5   four lines on the subject of 'Wine, Snow, and Poetry'. If your
poem proves to be good, I will give you a reward; if your poem
is bad, or you can't write at all...

PRECIOUS STREAM: Then I think my brother-in-law Wei will
excuse him because he needs a little perspiration!

10   WEI: No! I'll have him punished for his rudeness!

SILVER STREAM: Yes, that's right.

WANG: Do you hear, man?

HSIEH: Yes, Your Excellency! *(He gets up and calls.)*
Attendants, bring me pen and paper!

15   *(They are very surprised that he should give orders.)*

WANG: Really, how can he do this!

PRECIOUS STREAM: Why, this is how a true poet should act.
(To Hsieh.) If no one else will bring you what you want, I will.
(Before anyone can stop her, she takes her own chair to him,
20   *and prepares pen and paper for him.)*

HSIEH *(reading as he writes):*

Wine brings a double cheer if snow be here,
Snow takes a brighter white from song's delight.
Ah, but when cups abound,* and song is sweet,
25   And snow is falling round, the joy's complete.

Here you are, Your Excellency! *(He hands the piece of paper to*
Wang, who takes it.)

WANG *(reading aloud):*

Wine brings a double cheer if snow be here,
30   Snow takes a brighter white from song's delight.
Ah, but when cups abound, and song is sweet,
And snow is falling round, the joy's complete.

Well it is very good indeed!

SU: Yes, very good!

35   WEI: I don't think so. I could write a much better poem if I
had a little perspiration—no, not perspiration—*(He wipes his*

*when cups abound,   when there are many people drinking.

forehead again.) a little inspiration!

WANG *(to Hsieh):* All right. Thank you. You may go now. A reward will be given to you later on.

MADAM: I will make sure of that.

HSIEH *(bowing):* Many thanks, Your Excellency! *(He leaves.)*

WANG *(to his wife):* You see, my dear, our family needs a poet. When we want to enjoy an occasion like this we find that none of our family can write anything. This is why I am anxious to choose a husband for my dear Precious Stream. All whom I approve can write first-class poems.

PRECIOUS STREAM: My brother-in-law Wei used to show you very good poems before he married my sister.

WEI: I can still show you good poems if I am allowed.

SILVER STREAM: Yes, I am sure he can.

PRECIOUS STREAM: I should like to see you write them in front of me.

WEI: Impossible!

WANG: How can you ask him to do that? Anyway, these young men are also rich and come from noble families. You couldn't find anyone better than they.

MADAM: My dear child, you should obey your father. If you follow his wishes we shall all be grateful to you.

PRECIOUS STREAM: Since you all want me to marry one of those young men, may I know if every one of them is rich and noble?

WANG: Yes, certainly.

PRECIOUS STREAM: Is there not one or two among them not so rich and noble?

WANG *(quickly):* No, none! They are all equally rich and noble.

PRECIOUS STREAM: Then, dear Father, how can I choose? By choosing one I shall be unfair to the others. To be fair, I think I must refuse them all.

WANG: Oh! *(He puts his hand to his forehead.)*

MADAM: You seem to be cleverer than your father, dear child.

GOLDEN STREAM: Very clever indeed.

SILVER STREAM: Very silly.

WANG *(impatiently)*: I won't have this nonsense! Although I can't find out who is the best man, you must find out yourself
5 and make up your mind before your next birthday. We are going to have the wedding then.

PRECIOUS STREAM: Dear Father, you are the Prime Minister and therefore the cleverest man in the kingdom! *(Wang looks pleased.)* When the cleverest man in the kingdom cannot say
10 who is the most suitable, then how can I? I am a stupid young girl without any experience. How can I make a decision?

MADAM: That's true.

GOLDEN STREAM: Yes, dear Father, it's quite true.

SILVER STREAM: No! When I was young I was neither stupid
15 nor without experience.

WEI: Why don't you discuss this with your advisers?

SU: Nonsense! Our dear father-in-law will settle it sooner or later. In the meantime, let us not discuss the matter.

PRECIOUS STREAM: Thank you, dear brother-in-law!
20 WANG: I think I have a very good plan for settling it.

ALL: Good! How clever! And so soon!

WANG: Listen, my dear. On your birthday, the second of February, let us build a beautiful room raised above the garden and let all the men I have approved come beneath it. You will
25 be in the room with an embroidered ball. Throw the ball down and the one who catches it will be your husband.

PRECIOUS STREAM: Is that a wise way to settle such a problem?

WANG: It is the only way. And I am quite determined.
30 PRECIOUS STREAM: It will depend on luck.

WANG: It will not depend on luck. It will be the will of God. Let us leave.

(They all stand up. Tables and chairs are removed. The two Attendants go out followed by the two Maids and then followed
35 *by Madam.)*

SU *(to all)*: We have some business at home, if you will excuse us. *(He and Golden Stream go off.)*

WEI: Now, dear sister-in-law, let me give you a little advice.

PRECIOUS STREAM *(looking back and pointing to a corner):*
There is a rock ten times as large as the one used for our table.
I think you said just now that you could lift such a rock easily.
Now, will you please...   5

WEI *(taking hold of his wife's arm):*   I think we have some
important business waiting for us too. Good morning. *(He runs
away with his wife.)*

PRECIOUS STREAM: What *shall* I do? What *shall* I do? *(She
sits down in the middle of the stage on a chair.)* My maid, ask the   10
gardener, Hsieh Ping-Kuei, to come to me.

MAID: Yes, my lady. *(She calls Hsieh, who enters left and
kneels before Precious Stream.)*

HSIEH: What do you wish me to do, my lady?

PRECIOUS STREAM: Please stand up! My maid, bring a seat   15
for Mr. Hsieh. *(A seat is placed at the side.)*

HSIEH: How can I sit down before my lady?

PRECIOUS STREAM: The best of manners is obedience.

HSIEH *(sitting):*   Then I must thank you.

PRECIOUS STREAM *(to her Maid):*   My maid, go to my room   20
and fetch some fifty taels* of silver for me. Go as slowly as possible, and return as slowly as possible!

MAID: Yes, my lady. *(She goes very slowly.)*

PRECIOUS STREAM: Mr. Hsieh, I wish to help you, but first of
of all you must tell me about your family.   25

HSIEH: Thank you, my lady. Do you really want to know
about my family? Well, I am of a very poor family.

PRECIOUS STREAM: I already know that. I want to hear about
the members of your family.

HSIEH: My father and mother are both dead.   30

PRECIOUS STREAM: I see. Is there anyone else in your family?

HSIEH: I had a brother who died at five. I have no sister.

PRECIOUS STREAM: Did any one of your family marry?

HSIEH: Yes.

PRECIOUS STREAM *(surprised):*   Oh! Who?   35

HSIEH: Well, my father married my mother.

taels, Chinese ounce, a small weight.

PRECIOUS STREAM (*relieved*):   Of course! And your brother?

HSIEH: As he died at five he did not marry.

PRECIOUS STREAM: I see. Well—well—and did—did your parents have a daughter-in-law *at all*?

5   HSIEH: No, they had none.

PRECIOUS STREAM: Then you are not—not married?

HSIEH: Of course not!

PRECIOUS STREAM: Then I have something to tell you, but I find it difficult to do so. Well, do you understand riddles?*

10   HSIEH: A little.

PRECIOUS STREAM: The second of February will be my sixteenth birthday. I am going to marry the man who catches the embroidered ball which I shall throw down from a room above the garden. I have decided to make my own plans. I am thinking of a suitable person. Now this person, if you look far...

15   HSIEH (*continuing*):   He is a thousand miles away...

PRECIOUS STREAM: Yes, and if you look near...

HSIEH: Then he is before you!

PRECIOUS STREAM: Thank you! That is exactly what I mean.

20   HSIEH: If my lady wishes to give me such an honour I will do as she wishes.

PRECIOUS STREAM: Keep quiet, the maid is returning. Remember to come on the second of February.

HSIEH: The second of February.

25   MAID (*appearing*):   Here you are, my lady.

PRECIOUS STREAM (*not taking the money*):   Give it to Mr. Hsieh. (*The Maid does so.*)

HSIEH: Thank you! (*He gets up, bows, and goes.*) I'll never forget your kindness! The second of February. (*Precious Stream and her maid go off on the opposite side.*)

30   *The great day, the second of February, arrives. It is a fine day. The Prime Minister, Wang, gets up early in the morning and takes a walk in the garden, with two Attendants in front of him. An embroidered cloth is stretched on three sticks fastened to a table.*

35   *This acts as the garden room.*

WANG (*sitting down*):   Today I am going to take a son-in-law

*riddles, puzzling and difficult questions.

into my family. It is now nearly time to throw the ball, and I
must give the necessary instructions. *(He calls.)* Attendants!

ATTENDANTS: Yes, Your Excellency.

WANG: You must stay in the garden and guard the gate.
Admit only those young gentlemen whom you know I like. As   *5*
soon as the ball has been thrown, tell me the happy news at once.

ATTENDANTS: Yes, Your Excellency!

*(Wang goes; the Attendants move to one side. Four young
gentlemen, dressed in fine silk gowns, come from the right.)*

FIRST GENTLEMAN: Lady Precious Stream is as beautiful as   *10*
the flowers of May!

SECOND GENTLEMAN: The second of February is her wedding
day!

THIRD GENTLEMAN: The young gentlemen come here happy
and gay!   *15*

FOURTH GENTLEMAN: Here we have arrived. Let us knock
at the gate.

*(They turn and knock at the imaginary garden gate. Loud
knockings are heard.)*

FIRST ATTENDANT: Yes, I am coming. *(He comes forward and*   *20*
opens the double doors of the gate with both his hands.) Good
morning, my young lords. Have you gentlemen come to catch the
lucky ball?

ALL: Yes!

FIRST ATTENDANT *(showing the way)*: Come in, please.   *25*

*(They all enter the gate, bending their heads. The Second At-
tendant leads them to where they may sit on the grass.)*

ALL: Lady Precious Stream is coming!

*(They all stand up. Four Maids lead the way. Precious Stream
appears holding an embroidered ball and walks to the front of the* *30*
stage.)

PRECIOUS STREAM: Time flies, and today is the second of
February. Now that the important moment has come, I should
like it to be postponed. The garden must be rather crowded as
I can hear voices. I wonder if Hsieh Ping-Kuei is here. He pro- *35*
mised me that he would come, so I needn't worry. But to think
of throwing down the embroidered ball while the crowd looks

on makes me feel very afraid. I don't know how I shall do it.
My maids!

    MAIDS: Yes, my lady!

    PRECIOUS STREAM: Lead the way, please.

5   MAIDS: Yes, my lady!

*(They walk round the stage three times and stand at the two
sides of the garden room. Precious Stream is helped on the table
behind the embroidered cloth. Her head and shoulders can be seen
over it.)*

10   PRECIOUS STREAM *(looking at the crowd of Gentlemen)*:
Now I must look carefully! The princes are dressed in red and
the young nobles are dressed in green. Those in yellow are the
sons of rich merchants, and those in blue are the sons of great
land-owners!

15   *(Cheers from the crowd.)*

But I must find where Hsieh Ping-Kuei is standing. I have looked
from east to west, and now I must look from north to south. I
have looked everywhere for him, but he is nowhere to be seen.
When I gave him the silver I told him to come today. He pro-
20 mised he would. Oh, what should I do? I must go without throwing the ball.

    FIRST GENTLEMAN: No! You mustn't go back!

    SECOND GENTLEMAN: Throw the ball before you go, please!

    THIRD GENTLEMAN: How can you leave us?

25   FOURTH GENTLEMAN: I have been waiting the whole morning!

    PRECIOUS STREAM: Ah, I can see him coming from that corner
now! *(To the Gentlemen.)* Now, gentlemen, please come nearer
and listen to what I have to say. I want all of you to give me your
word of honour to support the man who, by the will of God, is
30 going to be my husband. Moreover, you must swear that you will
draw your swords against anyone who will not obey my instructions.

    ALL: We swear! We swear!

*(By this time Hsieh Ping-Kuei has appeared and is trying to
35 hide himself in a corner.)*

PRECIOUS STREAM: The marriage is to be arranged by the will of God, and we have to be true to this arrangement. *(She raises the ball.)* Now! Catch the ball!

(There are loud cries and she throws it to the corner where Hsieh is standing. He catches it before any of the other Gentlemen can even see it.)

FIRST GENTLEMAN: Where is the lucky ball?

SECOND GENTLEMAN: Who has got it?

THIRD GENTLEMAN: Has any one of you caught it?

FOURTH GENTLEMAN: I felt it passing above my head.

HSIEH *(coming out with the ball in his hand)*:   Here it is!

ALL: Oh! *(They all rush to him.)*

HSIEH: Stop! All of you! The man who dares to touch me will be struck dead.

FIRST GENTLEMAN: Who are you who dares to come among us?

SECOND GENTLEMAN: You are a servant of the house!

THIRD GENTLEMAN: No, even worse, a beggar!

FOURTH GENTLEMAN: That's right, I saw you begging in the street only a few months ago!

PRECIOUS STREAM: Gentlemen, remember that all of you have given your word of honour to me. Now, like good people, wish him and me good luck. *(She begins to come down from the room.)*

FIRST ATTENDANT *(to Second Attendant)*:   This is some real news. Let us go and tell His Excellency at once. *(They go.)*

ALL *(each holding his hands together)*:   Our very good wishes!

HSIEH: Thank you!

ALL *(going to Precious Stream)*:   Our very good wishes!

(Each holding his hands together, they bow very low.)

PRECIOUS STREAM: I thank you very much.

(His Excellency, Wang, comes running with two Attendants.)

WANG: Where is my new son-in-law? Where is my new son-in-law?

(He brings himself face to face with Hsieh, who meets him calmly.)

HSIEH *(nearly rubbing his nose on his future father-in-law's nose)*:   At your service, my dear Father-in-law!

(Wang, becoming angrier every moment, shakes his head and faints slowly but steadily into the arms of the Property Man who is ready to catch him.)

PRECIOUS STREAM *(fanning him with her arms):*   Oh, Father,
5 Father!

ALL *(doing the same):*   Oh, Your Excellency, Your Excellency!

WANG *(recovers; he sits on the ground):*   Oh my God!

PRECIOUS STREAM: Yes, dear Father, this is indeed the will of God.

ALL: The will of God!

WANG *(getting up and sitting on a chair)*:   But I won't accept this!   5

PRECIOUS STREAM: But, Father, aren't you glad? You said our family needed a poet, and now we have one! Your wish has come true!

WANG: We shall see if God will give me a different wish!

FIRST ATTENDANT *(to the Second Attendant)*:   It seems something terrible is about to happen. Let us go and tell Madam!

PRECIOUS STREAM *(to the Gentlemen)*:   Now, my brave Gentlemen, did you not swear that you would draw your swords against him who did not support the decision?

ALL: Yes, we did!

WANG *(to Precious Stream)*:   What! You have planned secretly against your own father!

PRECIOUS STREAM: I never thought that it would be you whom we should have to deal with.

WANG *(to the Gentlemen)*:   You fools! To think that I once liked you! I *am* a fool! Now get out, all of you!

(He goes and opens the gate and leads them out one by one, holding their left ears.)

(Madam, Golden Stream, Silver Stream, Su and Wei come with the two Attendants. After greetings, they are all seated except Precious Stream and Hsieh.)

MADAM *(to Precious Stream)*:   Why don't you sit down, my dear?

PRECIOUS STREAM: As my future husband is not given a seat, I can't sit down, dear Mother.

MADAM: Then be seated, both of you.

WANG: No! This is a Prime Minister's house, not a beggar's hut. How can he be allowed to sit down here?

MADAM: Dear, you are only making things worse. Let all of us sit down and talk over the matter, and see what is to be done.

WANG *(unwilling)*:   All right. Do what you like.

MADAM: Now be seated, please.

HSIEH: Thank you, Madam! *(He sits next to Wei, who turns away in disgust.)*

PRECIOUS STREAM: Thank you, dear Mother! And I am now waiting for your instructions, dear Father.

WANG: I have no instructions for you! It is he whom I want to deal with. Tell me, on what conditions will you let her be free?

(All look at Hsieh, who does not answer.)

WEI *(to Hsieh):*   Look here, man. *(No answer.)* Say, my friend! *(No answer.)* Hullo, Hsieh Ping-Kuei! *(Still no answer.)* Mr. Hsieh Ping-Kuei.

HSIEH: What is your wish, my great General?   5

WEI: Don't be angry, my—eh—Mr. Hsieh. You know that Lady Precious Stream cannot marry you, a beg—, I mean a poor man. I quite understand that this is a great chance for you, and that you must have a good price before you will give her up.

HSIEH *(fiercely):*   I don't know what you mean!   10

SILVER STREAM: You can't make my husband afraid! Frighten him back, my dear!

WEI: Be quiet dear! *(To Hsieh again.)* I mean that if you will give up Lady Precious Stream without talking about it, I am sure my father-in-law is willing to give you, say...   15

SILVER STREAM: One hundred taels of silver!

(Hsieh is getting angry.)

WEI: No, say two hundred.

SILVER STREAM: Not a bit more!

(Hsieh turns away in anger.)   20

WANG: I am a just and generous man. I will offer you five hundred taels.

SILVER STREAM: Oh!

WEI: Now, be sensible, my man. *(No answer.)* Well, how much do you want, my—eh—Mr. Hsieh?   25

HSIEH *(firmly):*   I want nothing from you, sir. Even millions cannot make me give up Lady Precious Stream. The decision lies with her. If she thinks that I am not worthy of her, and that this is but a sad mistake, just let her say so and I will go away without taking anything from you.   30

PRECIOUS STREAM: Beautiful!

SU: It's quite right!

MADAM: Dear, dear!

WANG: My dear daughter, you know that to me you are dearer than all. Now, tell him you cannot let him marry you.   35

WEI: And if—eh—Mr. Hsieh refuses to take any money,

then the five hundred taels you promised, dear Father-in-law, ought to be given to me as a reward for helping you.

SILVER STREAM: Of course Father will reward you, dear!

PRECIOUS STREAM: I am sorry to rob you of your reward. I will
5 not give up my husband. To my sister I am worth one hundred taels and to my brother-in-law only two hundred. To my father who says that he loves me above all, I am worth only five hund-dred...

WANG: No. I was prepared to offer one thousand...

10 PRECIOUS STREAM: Thank you, Father! I see I am worth more now. You seem to think that one would prefer to have, let us say, a thousand taels rather than to have me! Here is the man who refuses to take millions and prefers me instead. Shall I be so ungrateful as to let him go and to remain with those who
15 value me so little? No, Father, I refuse!

GOLDEN STREAM: So would I!

MADAM *(moved)*:   Dear, dear!

SU: Very noble!

SILVER STREAM: Very silly!

20 WEI: It's too bad. My five hundred taels gone!

WANG *(immediately)*:   Be quiet! This is too much! If you insist on marrying him, all I can say is this: that a beggar girl is going to marry a beggar, and remains one! You need not expect any money from me—no, not even a penny.

25 ALL: Oh!

HSIEH: I have already said that I won't take anything from you!

PRECIOUS STREAM: No, Father, not a beggar girl to a beggar, but a working girl to a worker! We both can work.

30 WANG: You! Work! Impossible!

SILVER STREAM: Don't you think that it will dirty your beautiful silk dresses?

PRECIOUS STREAM: No, because I will not wear them!

(She begins to take off her outer silk dress while all the rest
35 *of the family crowd round her to hide her. They sit down as soon as this is over, and she is now in a plain black gown.)*

There is an old saying: 'A good son will not depend upon

his father's wealth; and a good daughter will not depend upon
her family for clothes.' *(She offers him the clothes. It is a Property Man who receives them.)* And here are the jewels, too.
(She takes off her jewels rapidly and gives them to her father.)

MADAM: Oh, dear, don't!   5

GOLDEN STREAM: My poor sister!

SU: A brave girl!

SILVER STREAM: I wonder how they will manage to live?

WEI: They will soon die of hunger.

WANG *(still angry)*:   Are you going to leave us and follow   10
that man? Probably you will return to me when you find that
you are hungry!

PRECIOUS STREAM: That will not happen. If I come back to
see you, dear Father, it will be when we are more important than
any of you!   15

WEI: Don't dream!

SILVER STREAM: Wake up, please!

PRECIOUS STREAM: To be rich or poor is the will of God.
You can never tell what may happen.

WANG: I can tell that you will be poor and miserable. But   20
don't come to me for help.

MADAM: Don't listen to what your father says, dear. We
shall always be glad to help you. But you are not really going
to leave us for ever, are you?

GOLDEN STREAM: Please don't, dear sister!   25

PRECIOUS STREAM: I am afraid I shall have to. My place is at
my husband's side, whatever may happen.

WANG: But I am sure you will be glad to leave him very soon.

PRECIOUS STREAM: I call upon all of you here as witnesses.
My husband and I will not come back to the Prime Minister's   30
house unless we are rich and successful. *(To Hsieh.)* Now, will
you come and say good-bye to your father-in-law?

HSIEH: Yes. *(He holds his hands together and bows to Wang
who turns away.)*

PRECIOUS STREAM: And to your mother-in-law. *(Hsieh does   35
the same.)* No! You must kneel down to her, to show that you
respect her. *(Hsieh kneels.)* Again, please! *(He does so.)*

MADAM *(pleased)*: I am sure you will make a very good, obedient husband!

PRECIOUS STREAM: To your sisters-in-law, too! *(Hsieh holds his hands together and bows to them.)*

5   GOLDEN STREAM *(returning the action)*: I wish you both good luck!

SILVER STREAM *(turning away)*: It is getting very late now.

PRECIOUS STREAM: And to your brothers-in-law! *(Hsieh does the same.)*

10   SU: I wish you every happiness and success!

HSIEH: Thank you very much. I won't forget your kindness!

WEI *(turning away)*: I think we ought to be going now.

PRECIOUS STREAM: Now stand aside and wait a moment for me. *(To her father.)* My dear Father, your humble daughter,
15   Precious Stream, pays her respects...

WANG: No, you needn't think of me as your father!

PRECIOUS STREAM *(charmingly)*: Then I must, at least, thank you for your share in my birth! *(She kneels and bows forward.)*

WANG: It was a mere accident.

20   SILVER STREAM: And a sad one, too!

PRECIOUS STREAM *(kneeling before her mother)*: My dear, dear Mother, I can never thank you enough! And I shall miss you very much. *(She cries.)*

MADAM *(getting up from her seat and putting her arms round*
25   *her daughter)*: My dear, remember that your mother will always be ready to help you.

PRECIOUS STREAM: No, thank you all the same, Mother. I won't have any help from the Wang family.

SILVER STREAM: 'A daughter who has married and left her
30   family is like water poured into the street', as the old saying goes.

GOLDEN STREAM: Don't say that, sister!

PRECIOUS STREAM: It's quite all right, and I hope she will realize some day that she is like the water poured into the street.
35   *(She curtsies* to them.)* Good-bye, my dear sisters!

*to curtsy, to bend the knees and lower the body. A man bows but a woman curtsies.

GOLDEN STREAM: Don't say good-bye, my dear sister! Surely you will allow me to call on you?

PRECIOUS STREAM: That depends.

SILVER STREAM: Good-bye, dear sister, and I do hope we shall soon meet again, when you are sorry for what you have done.   5

PRECIOUS STREAM: Never! *(Curtsies to Su and Wei.)* Good-bye, my brothers-in-law.

SU *(bowing):* Good-bye for now. I will be at your wedding.

PRECIOUS STREAM: It will be a very simple one, and if you are busy...   10

SU: No, no, I must be there.

WEI: I regret to say I am rather busy now, so if you will excuse me...

PRECIOUS STREAM: Certainly, we do not want to force anyone to come! Good-bye, and I hope never to see your... beautiful   15
face again. *(To Hsieh.)* Now let us leave here for ever and prepare for the wedding.

HSIEH: I will always honour you.

PRECIOUS STREAM: And I will obey you!

HSIEH: I will protect you!   20

PRECIOUS STREAM: I will *love* you!

(They go out.)

WANG: Let us go.

(They go out one after the other.)

Act II

The marriage was not a failure. Precious Stream and Hsieh re-
fused to accept any help from the Wang family. Because of this
they were poor but they were happy. They were very brave, espe-
cially Precious Stream. Although she came from a rich and noble
5 *family she was willing to work hard and became a very good and*
happy wife. Let us see what happens.

We are in an open space outside the city. There is a kind of cave
where Precious Stream and Hsieh live. We must imagine that the
stage is the open space in front of the cave as well as the inside of
10 *the cave. If possible, we can show a twisting road on the little hill*
which leads to the cave. There is nothing else on the stage. The
audience should use their imagination.

Two soldiers enter from the right: one carries a small sack of
rice, the other has a small bundle of firewood. They go to the door
15 *of the cave.*

FIRST SOLDIER: Here we are.

SECOND SOLDIER: Yes, I think this is the place.

FIRST SOLDIER: Let us knock at the door. *(He knocks.)* Is
there anyone at home?

20 A VOICE *(off stage):* Yes, I am coming.
(Precious Stream appears from the right. She is simply but care-
fully dressed.)

PRECIOUS STREAM: If you are rich, even relatives from far
away come to visit you. If you are poor, even the closest relatives
25 will not come near you. Since I married Hsieh Ping-Kuei, we
have had very few visitors. But I just heard a strange knock at
the door. *(She calls out.)* Who is it?

FIRST SOLDIER: We have brought some firewood and rice
from our eldest brother, Hsieh.

30 PRECIOUS STREAM: And where is Hsieh himself?

SECOND SOLDIER: He will be back very soon.

PRECIOUS STREAM: Thank you. *(She opens the door.)* Please bring in what you have brought.

(They enter.)

FIRST SOLDIER: Here is half a ton of firewood.   *5*

PRECIOUS STREAM *(finding a place for it):* Put it here, please. *(The First Soldier puts the firewood down. The Property Man takes it away immediately.)*

SECOND SOLDIER: Here is a quarter of a ton of rice.

PRECIOUS STREAM *(finding another place for the rice):* Put it   *10* here, please. *(The Second Soldier puts the rice down. The Property Man takes it away immediately.)* As your eldest brother, Hsieh, is not at home, I cannot ask you to stay and drink a cup of tea. Please excuse me.

FIRST SOLDIER: Please do not worry.   *15*

SECOND SOLDIER: Thank you all the same.

PRECIOUS STREAM: Thank you for bringing the firewood and the rice. I will not keep you.

FIRST SOLDIER: Don't mention it. Good-bye.

SECOND SOLDIER: We are happy to help. Good-bye.   *20*

PRECIOUS STREAM: Good-bye. *(The soldiers leave. She closes the door, sits on a chair and pretends to sew.)*

A VOICE *(off stage):* Look out, a horse is coming!

(Hsieh Ping-Kuei arrives on horseback. He shows this by waving with his right hand. He is dressed as an officer in the army. To *25* *show that he is riding he walks from side to side. He moves to the front of the stage and speaks to the audience, holding the whip across his chest.)*

HSIEH: To one who is just married, an hour away from his home seems to be three years. So I feel I have been absent from *30* my home for a very long time. I have some important news for my wife and must go home quickly. *(He waves his whip and turns round.)* Here is my poor cave which I consider to be better than a grand palace. *(He calls.)* My dear third sister, will you kindly open the door?   *35*

PRECIOUS STREAM *(getting up):* Is that you, my lord and master, Hsieh? *(She opens the door.)*

(Hsieh gets off his horse, drops his whip and goes in.)

HSIEH: Yes, I have come back with some important news.

PRECIOUS STREAM *(giving him her seat and sitting at his side)*:
Never mind about the news; the most important thing is, do you
want something to eat and drink?

HSIEH: Thank you. I have had a good dinner at the camp.

PRECIOUS STREAM: So! That's why the two soldiers brought
us half a ton of firewood and a quarter of a ton of rice!

HSIEH: Yes, that is part of the news, too. It is payment in ad-
vance of my pay, and we needn't worry about our food any
more!

PRECIOUS STREAM: Good news indeed!

HSIEH: I have just been appointed an officer of considerable
rank.

PRECIOUS STREAM: That's fairly good!

HSIEH: You don't seem to be very excited about the good
news.

PRECIOUS STREAM: Oh, yes, I am rather glad that you are
now beginning to progress. But this is only a beginning. To me,
my husband ought not to be satisfied until he is more important
than all other men!

HSIEH: I will do my best for you, dear.

PRECIOUS STREAM: Very good! And what else do you want to
tell me? I see that you are worried about something.

HSIEH: Well, as I am now in government service I cannot
just do as I like. I am ordered abroad...

PRECIOUS STREAM: 'A man's ambition cannot be limited by
space!' as the old saying goes. You needn't be afraid to tell me
that you must leave me for a time, though we have been married
for a month only.

HSIEH *(still uneasy)*: But the fact is—is—well, it is a very
long journey. We are going to the Western Regions.

PRECIOUS STREAM *(surprised)*: Oh! It is a long and danger-
ous journey even in peaceful times; and now we are at war with
them.

HSIEH: That's why I am going.

PRECIOUS STREAM: Even those who go to the Western Regions as friends seldom return... I mean, seldom return satisfied.

HSIEH: No! They never return at all!

PRECIOUS STREAM: And are you going there as their enemy?

HSIEH: Our aim is to conquer them.

PRECIOUS STREAM: When do you start?

HSIEH: Very soon.   5

PRECIOUS STREAM: Then I must prepare some winter clothes for you, because you may have to stay there over the New Year.

HSIEH: You needn't make any preparations for me. I have something more to tell you.

PRECIOUS STREAM: Then tell me at once!   10

HSIEH: It is very difficult to tell you at once.

PRECIOUS STREAM (*forcing a smile through her tears*):   Then tell me little by little. I shall not object.

HSIEH: The date of our going is fixed.

PRECIOUS STREAM (*anxiously*):   When?   15

HSIEH: Well, do you understand riddles?

PRECIOUS STREAM: A little.

HSIEH: If I say the date is far, far away...

PRECIOUS STREAM (*forcing another smile*):   A hundred years away!   20

HSIEH: And if I say the date is quite, quite near at hand...

PRECIOUS STREAM: Today! (*She hides her face in her hands.*)

HSIEH (*going to her and trying to calm her*):   Try not to worry. Wouldn't you be glad to see me return victorious, a general on horseback? That is something to which you may look forward!   25

PRECIOUS STREAM: But to think we have only been married for a month, and you are leaving me today! So unexpectedly, too! Why did you apply for such a position?

HSIEH: I didn't apply for it, it was given to me.

PRECIOUS STREAM: How?   30

HSIEH (*sitting*):   You know people have been talking about a monster with red hair which has been eating travellers in a wood nearby. Well, I thought I ought to do something. I went to the wood this morning and shot the monster. It was only a big tiger.

PRECIOUS STREAM: A big tiger! And you say 'only'.   35

HSIEH: Yes. I was quite disappointed.

PRECIOUS STREAM (*forgetting her troubles for a minute*):   How wonderful! Now, my dear, tell me how you did it!

HSIEH: Eh—eh—there is very little to tell. I went there, I saw a tiger, I shot it, that's all!

PRECIOUS STREAM: 'I went there, I saw a tiger, I shot it!' How brave! How admirable!

HSIEH: Nonsense! While others say it was admirable I thought it very disappointing. Shooting an ordinary tiger when expecting a monster is as disappointing as shooting a bird when hunting a tiger! And the worst of it is that people think it was so wonderful.

PRECIOUS STREAM: And they make trouble, too!

HSIEH: Yes, terrible trouble. They actually carried me to the Governor, and I was appointed a captain. I found that Generals Wei and Su, our brothers-in-law, are the commanders-in-chief, and I was ordered to join the First Company immediately!

PRECIOUS STREAM *(faintly)*: Immediately!

HSIEH: Yes. I had to beg him to allow me to come back to bid you a quick good-bye. I am afraid I have already stayed too long.

PRECIOUS STREAM: Oh, no! You mustn't leave me like this!

HSIEH *(getting up and preparing to go)*: I am afraid I must. I was ordered to start at once. Don't worry about me, the commanders-in-chief are our brothers-in-law, you see!

PRECIOUS STREAM *(getting up too)*: I am more worried than ever on hearing that Wei is your chief. I don't trust him at all, and I hope you will take the greatest care of yourself.

HSIEH: You needn't worry at all, for he is not going. He's staying behind to control the supplies and the paying of the soldiers. I have arranged for my pay to be given to you regularly in the form of rice and firewood, and he promised to arrange that. General Su will follow me with the rest of the soldiers in a short time.

PRECIOUS STREAM: That is excellent! I know how to deal with Wei, and I am relieved to hear that our brother-in-law Su is going to follow you soon.

A VOICE *(off stage)*: Dear eldest brother Hsieh, the soldiers are waiting for you!

HSIEH *(calling out)*:   Thank you! I will come at once. *(To Precious Stream.)* I must go now. My dear third sister, allow me to bid you good-bye. *(He holds his hands together, bows respect-fully and she curtsies.)*

PRECIOUS STREAM *(following her husband)*:   I must see you get on your horse.

(Hsieh goes out of the cave, picks up the whip, and gets on his horse.)

HSIEH: My dear third sister, good-bye!

PRECIOUS STREAM: Good-bye! I must see you ride along the road.

HSIEH *(going around the stage three times)*:   You will take care of yourself, won't you?

PRECIOUS STREAM: Of course!

A VOICE *(off stage)*:   Aren't you coming, dear eldest brother Hsieh? We are waiting for you.

HSIEH *(calling out)*:   I am coming! *(To Precious Stream.)* Now please go back, my dear third sister!

PRECIOUS STREAM: Do let me follow you for another short distance!

HSIEH: No, no! I can't bear to leave you, but we must part sooner or later. The road is rough, and you are already tired. Please go back and rest.

PRECIOUS STREAM: No, no! I must see you off from the camp.

HSIEH: Impossible! That is too far for you.

PRECIOUS STREAM: I must.

A VOICE *(off stage)*:   We are starting, dear eldest brother Hsieh.

HSIEH *(calling out)*:   I am coming! *(Pointing to a corner be-hind Precious Stream.)* There is your sister coming. *(Precious Stream turns back and Hsieh then rides away.)*

PRECIOUS STREAM: Oh, he has gone! *(She weeps and goes off.)*

More than nine months have passed. Precious Stream has re-ceived very little of the things that were promised. She would have suffered from hunger and cold had she not worked to keep herself. First, she heard the news that Hsieh Ping-Kuei had been killed by

*the enemy, and then she received the official report that he was in-
deed lost. Wei refused to give Precious Stream more rice and
firewood because Hsieh was supposed to be dead. Madam Wang,
hearing the news, comes to her daughter to offer help.*

*5   Precious Stream comes from the right. She is in her ordinary
working clothes with a cloth tied round her head, to show she is
ill.*

PRECIOUS STREAM: When I was on my bed, taking a little rest,
I suddenly heard someone knocking at my door. It is perhaps
10 some neighbours who have come to see if I am well. Since my
husband left, I have had no news from him at all.

VOICE *(outside):* Open the door, please, Lady Precious
Stream. Madam, your mother, has come to visit you.

PRECIOUS STREAM *(frightened):* Ah! This will kill me! How
15 can I face my mother? Oh, my dear, dear Mother! *(She opens the
door, goes out, and puts her arms round her mother.)*

MADAM: My dear Precious Stream!

PRECIOUS STREAM: My Mother!

MADAM: My daughter!

20 PRECIOUS STREAM: How I have longed to see you, Mother!

MADAM: And I to see you too! But what a change! You have
now become a thin, hollow-faced, hungry-looking, ordinary
person! Oh, I cannot bear this! When you were with us you were
always attended by servants. When you were tired of staying in
25 your room, you could have a little walk in the garden. And now,
no servants, no nice room, no garden! How can you bear it? And
the worst of it is you have no company. This cave cannot keep
out the cold. How can you remain in such a place, you, who
are the favourite daughter of His Excellency the Prime Minister!
30 *(She cries.)*

PRECIOUS STREAM: Dear Mother, please don't cry. Listen
to your daughter. My eldest and second sisters married great and
rich men. But your third daughter has married a poor man!
It takes all kinds of people to make a world, so there is no use
35 complaining. If everybody were to be an official, who would dig
the ground?

MADAM: I am not complaining, my dear; I only regret that

my husband has been unkind. He has two kinds of treatment for his three daughters. He used to say that you, to him, were dearer than all, yet he treats you and your husband badly. I love the other two daughters, but I love you the most. I am getting old and I have aged greatly this year. Seeing you makes me feel *5* young again. I feel fresh and strong like a dry, fading plant after the rains of spring.

PRECIOUS STREAM: Dear Mother, allow me to kneel down and pay my respects to you.

MADAM *(stopping her)*:   No, you mustn't stand on ceremony. *10*

PRECIOUS STREAM *(kneeling down and bowing forward)*:   Your daughter has caused you too much suffering to be pardoned! Let her kneel before you to beg forgiveness!

MADAM *(taking her into her arms again)*:   Don't, my darling. It is your forgiveness that we should all beg. *(To the Servants* *15* *attending her.)* Attendants, come nearer and pay your respects to Lady Precious Stream!

ALL: Our respects to you, Lady Precious Stream.

(The Servants kneel on one knee.)

PRECIOUS STREAM *(returning their salute with a curtsy)*: *20* Thank you. Please don't stand on ceremony.

MADAM: Now you may go and have a rest, but return in a short time.

ALL: Thank you, Madam. *(They leave.)*

PRECIOUS STREAM: Oh, dear Mother, how can you come to *25* our humble cave?

MADAM: I have heard that you are hungry and cold, and you are not well. So I wanted to see you and the place where you are living.

PRECIOUS STREAM *(stopping her)*:   Oh, no! My humble cave *30* is not good enough for you.

MADAM: Nonsense! I must go in and see what kind of a life you are leading.

PRECIOUS STREAM: It is a small miserable hole and would only make you feel uncomfortable. *35*

MADAM *(firmly)*:   The place where my dear daughter can live for nearly a year is at least good enough for me to visit!

PRECIOUS STREAM *(giving in)*:   Then let me go in first and
have the place tidied for you.

MADAM: No, I want to see it just as it is. Lead the way, my
darling.

5   *(They turn and enter the cave.)*

PRECIOUS STREAM: Be careful of the steps, dear Mother!

MADAM *(looking around)*:   So this is your place! Oh, you
silly girl, why did you leave your beautiful room and come to
this miserable cave? How could you?

10   PRECIOUS STREAM *(offering her a broken chair)*:   Make yourself comfortable in this poor chair, dear Mother. I am afraid I
have no tea to offer you, except some poor rice. *(She takes a
small bowl and gives it to Madam.)*

MADAM *(taking it and putting it down)*:   Why did you give up
15   the good things you enjoyed for this poor stuff. How could you?
Now, sit down yourself.

PRECIOUS STREAM *(sitting on the left side)*:   Thank you, dear
Mother! After those rich things, this plain food seemed to be
very good to me.

20   MADAM: You are not eating enough. That's why you are ill.

PRECIOUS STREAM: Indeed it is not because of food. The
wicked Wei told me that my husband had been killed! It was
this news that made me ill.

MADAM: This news may be false, darling.

25   PRECIOUS STREAM: Oh, yes! I don't believe it at all. But, still,
it makes me feel sad. And Father sends people to persuade me
to marry again, which makes me feel worse.

MADAM *(angry)*:   The wicked old man! He'll be very sorry
when I've finished talking to him tonight!

30   PRECIOUS STREAM: Oh, no! Please don't quarrel with Father
on *my* account.

MADAM: Very well, then. He has to thank you if I don't
punish him. How are you feeling now?

PRECIOUS STREAM: You see I am already feeling much bet-
35   ter at the sight of you!

MADAM: But this is not the place in which to get well. Now
be reasonable, and come back with your mother to our house

where you need not worry about anything. You will have plenty
to eat and plenty to wear.

PRECIOUS STREAM: No, dear Mother. I made a promise to
Father that I would not return to the Prime Minister's house
until we were quite rich.   5

MADAM: But you will die of hunger if you stay here.

PRECIOUS STREAM: I'd rather be hungry here than go back.

MADAM: Foolish child!

PRECIOUS STREAM: I am too proud to break my promise.

MADAM: Nonsense! Now tell me, when did you last hear from your husband?

5   PRECIOUS STREAM *(clearing her throat)*:   I have not heard from him since he left. The official news said that there was a general defeat, after which all the soldiers were ordered to retreat through the Pass as quickly as possible. The army was in great confusion, and many officers who went to the front were

10   killed before they could return through the Pass. Not long ago, when the troops of the Western Regions had gone, our search party returned with the report that my husband was among those who were killed.

MADAM: Oh, my dear, let us hope that he has escaped some-

15   how, and will return safe and sound!

PRECIOUS STREAM: Thank you, dear Mother! But I hoped he would return victorious.

MADAM: You can't expect that now.

PRECIOUS STREAM: To return as a deserter* or an escaped

20   prisoner would be worse than not to return at all!

MADAM *(surprised)*:   Oh, brave girl. What is to be done now? I think the best way for you is to come back with me, and if your father tries to say anything against you he will have *me* to deal with.

25   PRECIOUS STREAM *(determined)*:   No! I am afraid you'll have to go back alone, dear Mother. And if Father talks about me, tell him to think of me as dead or, better still, regard me as never having been born.

MADAM: Don't be stupid. Don't mind your father. Come to

30   your mother! The place where your mother goes is the place where you should go. Your mother will protect you. No one will dare to say a word against you!

PRECIOUS STREAM: But I can't go with you.

MADAM: Then since you refuse to go with me, I will stay here

35   with you instead.

*deserter,   here means a soldier who leaves the army without permission.

PRECIOUS STREAM *(frightened)*:   Oh, no! This is no place for you to stay.

MADAM: I am determined. The place where my darling lives is at least good enough for me to stay a few nights.

PRECIOUS STREAM *(worried, walking about the stage)*:   I can-   5
not allow this! She cannot stay here!

MADAM: You can't force me to go.

(The Servants return. They stand quietly outside the cave.)

PRECIOUS STREAM: The servants have come back. I think you ought to go now, dear Mother.   10

MADAM: No! Attendants, bring in the silver, the rice, and the clothes which you have brought with you.

ATTENDANTS: Yes, Madam. *(They enter the cave and produce several small parcels from their sleeves.)*

MADAM: Give them to Lady Precious Stream.   15

ATTENDANTS *(doing so)*:   Yes, Madam. These are for you, Lady Precious Stream.

PRECIOUS STREAM: No, Mother! I won't take anything from the Wang family.

MADAM: Put them down there! *(To Precious Stream.)* Non-   20
sense! They are presents from me to you. They have nothing to do with your father. Besides, when I am staying with you we shall need a little money to buy some extra food. You can't expect me to live on poor rice all the time.

PRECIOUS STREAM: But, dear Mother, you can't stay here   25
with me!

MADAM: Can't I? You will see. *(To the Servants.)* All of you may go home now, for I am going to stay a few days here with Lady Precious Stream.

ALL: Yes, Madam. *(The Attendants go out of the cave and*   30
prepare to leave.)

PRECIOUS STREAM *(to all)*:   Wait, please. *(Aside to herself.)* What shall I do? *(She taps her forehead with her fingers.)* Ah, I have it! *(To Madam.)* Well, Mother, I have changed my mind. I agree to return with you rather than let you stay here with me.   35

MADAM *(pleased)*:   Wonderful! Then come at once! *(She gets up and starts off.)*

PRECIOUS STREAM *(assisting her mother):* Mind the steps, Mother. *(They come out of the cave.)* Oh, Mother, I forgot something.

MADAM: What is it, darling?

5   PRECIOUS STREAM: I forgot to lock the cave door.

MADAM: Never mind. I will tell the servants to lock it for you.

PRECIOUS STREAM: And I forgot to put the silver, the rice, and the clothes in a safe place.

MADAM: They won't be lost if the cave door is locked.

10   PRECIOUS STREAM: But the rats. They will eat the rice and destroy the clothes.

MADAM: They are worth very little. I can afford to get more.

PRECIOUS STREAM: I can't allow anything from my dear mother to be destroyed. I won't be long.

15   MADAM: Then be quick!

PRECIOUS STREAM *(running into the cave and closing the door quickly):* Mother, I am not going back with you! And for my disobedience I am kneeling inside the cave. *(She kneels and cries aloud.)*

20   MADAM *(realizing her daughter's plan):* Oh, my darling! How could you? *(She cries too.)*

PRECIOUS STREAM: Dear Mother, though I remain in the cave, my heart goes with you!

MADAM *(crying):* Oh, my poor daughter!

25   PRECIOUS STREAM *(crying):* Oh, my poor, dear Mother! *(Madam goes off.)*

Act III

We are coming to a strange land known as the Western Regions.
The customs here are different from those of China; the women
here wear long gowns, while the men wear short coats and have
their trousers showing. Their appearance, too, is unusual. All,
male and female, have red hair, green eyes, large noses, and hairy   5
hands. To most people these things seem quite unbelievable.

The stage is the court of His Majesty the King of the Western
Regions. The audience should imagine the furniture and decora-
tions of the court to be as strange as the people of the Western
Regions.   10

The strangest thing of all is that His Majesty the King of the
Western Regions is Hsieh Ping-Kuei! He is still alive. After con-
quering the Western Regions, he has made himself their King.

It has been arranged that a royal wedding will take place the
next day. Hsieh Ping-Kuei is to marry a foreign princess who has   15
helped him in his battles. It is said that he is not very willing to
marry this princess. People wonder why he should not be anxious
to marry such a beautiful girl. But we all know the reason why
Hsieh is not happy.

Hsieh Ping-Kuei appears, following a big procession of Atten-   20
dants and Courtiers, or people of the Court. He is dressed in
a magnificent robe and wears a beautifully decorated crown. When
we first see him we cannot believe that he is the man we knew ear-
lier on. Hsieh, as we knew him, was a clean-shaven man, but His
Majesty has a thick black beard over a foot long! However, when   25
we look closely we can see by the way he moves and from his face
that he is indeed Hsieh Ping-Kuei.

Eighteen years have passed since we last saw him. Time has,
of course, changed him in some ways, and so have his clothes! He
wore an officer's uniform the last time we saw him. Now he is   30
dressed in a robe that would make even a beggar look like a king.

HSIEH: By the help of the Royal Princess I have now become your humble servant, the King of the Western Regions. *(He is helped to sit down on a chair behind a table.)* I have been away from my home for eighteen years. There are two things
5   I want to do very much: to return to my wife, Precious Stream, and to take revenge on Wei, the Tiger General, because he tried to have me killed. When I returned victorious, after the others had been defeated, General Wei pretended to be happy at my victory. He gave a big dinner party in his camp and made me
10   drunk with strong wine. Then he tied me to a horse and sent it galloping towards the enemy. Luckily I was rescued by the Princess, who cut me loose and later helped me to conquer all the Western Regions. She wishes to marry me and I cannot possibly refuse after what she has done for me. But I have postponed the
15   wedding again and again. Now, at last, I have to marry her. Everyone in the kingdom is happy that we are getting married. I alone do not look forward to it. Several times, I have tried to tell her that I am already married, but I can't bear to make her unhappy. What shall I do? What *shall* I do?
20   *(An old Priest appears.)*

PRIEST: Hsieh Ping-Kuei is unfaithful! Hsieh Ping-Kuei is unfaithful!

FIRST ATTENDANT *(kneeling before Hsieh)*:   I beg to report that a wild goose is flying over the palace making strange sounds.
25   HSIEH *(getting down from his seat)*:   Show me where it is.

PRIEST: Hsieh Ping-Kuei is unfaithful! Hsieh Ping-Kuei is unfaithful!

FIRST ATTENDANT *(pointing to the Priest)*: There is the bird, Your Majesty!
30   HSIEH *(to himself)*:   This is strange. It seems to be saying that I am unfaithful. This is indeed a bad sign. *(To the Attendants.)* Attendants, bring me my bow and arrows.

ATTENDANTS: Yes, Your Majesty!

(The First Attendant presents him with a bow only.)
35   HSIEH *(to himself again)*:   I have never before heard a wild goose making sounds which seem to be like the words of a human being. *(He appears to shoot an arrow from his bow.)* With

my bow and arrow I shoot it. *(He shoots.)* There!

(The Priest goes off, leaving a letter on the ground.)

FIRST ATTENDANT *(picking it up and kneeling before Hsieh)*:
Your Majesty, I found this piece of cloth on that bird.

HSIEH: Hand it to me.   5

FIRST ATTENDANT *(handing it)*:   Yes, Your Majesty!

HSIEH *(reading it)*:   Ah! 'Precious Stream presents her respects to her unfaithful...' Oh, my dear wife! I can't stop the tears
flowing from my eyes! *(To all.)* Courtiers and Attendants,
leave me for a while! *(They all go.)* The words on the cloth, torn   10
from her skirt, are written with her blood! *(He reads the letter
again.)* Every line, every word is written in blood! It says:
'Precious Stream presents her respects to her unfaithful husband,
Hsieh Ping-Kuei. She wishes to tell him that since he went away
she has been alone and suffering in the cave. If he returns imme-   15
diately, they may meet each other once more. If he delays, even
for a few days, they may never see each other again!' *(He looks
towards the east.)* Far, far away, there is my home, my sweet
home! Oh, my dear, dear Precious Stream, my dear, dear wife!
I must go back in time to see you. Let me think of some plan.   20
(He taps his forehead with his fingers.) Ah, I must do it! I must
do it no matter what happens! *(The Attendants reappear.)* Attendants!

ATTENDANTS: Yes, Your Majesty!

HSIEH: Ask Her Highness the Royal Princess to come to   25
Court.

ATTENDANTS: Yes, Your Majesty!

THE FIRST ATTENDANT *(going to the right and calling loudly)*:
His Majesty requests the presence of Her Highness the Royal
Princess!   30

VOICE *(off stage)*:   I will obey!

*(Her Highness the Royal Princess of the Western Regions
wears a military uniform but we can still see that she is a very
charming woman. There are four small, beautifully embroidered
flags fastened to her back; two long feathers stick out of her   35
helmet. There is a white fur round her neck. Four Maids come
on before her.)*

PRINCESS *(to the audience)*:　I am your humble maid, the Royal Princess of the Western Regions. His Majesty has commanded me to go to Court. *(To her Maids.)* My maids, lead the way to the Court. *(They walk on and stop before Hsieh.)*

5　Your humble maid, the Royal Princess of the Western Regions, offers her respects to Your Majesty!

HSIEH:　Don't stand on ceremony.

PRINCESS:　Thank you!

HSIEH:　Please sit down.

10　PRINCESS:　Thank you, Your Majesty. May I know what important matter Your Majesty wishes to discuss with me?

HSIEH:　No! There is nothing important to discuss. You have been working very hard, checking and looking after our soldiers. Now I want to have a big dinner in your honour.

15　PRINCESS *(very pleased)*:　This would indeed be a great honour! Allow me to serve Your Majesty with wine. *(To her Maids.)* My maids!

MAIDS:　Yes, Your Highness!

PRINCESS:　Prepare wine for me!

20　MAIDS:　Yes, Your Highness!

HSIEH:　Oh, no! I will not let you trouble yourself. Attendants!

ATTENDANTS:　Yes, Your Majesty!

HSIEH *(to the Princess)*:　Let me have the pleasure of serving

25　you. *(The First Attendant presents him with wine and two cups on a tray. He serves the Princess, who drinks.)* I am very happy to be here, drinking with you but I am worried that the neighbouring state will attack us.

PRINCESS *(finding the subject the one she likes the most)*:　I

30　beg Your Majesty not to worry about the invasion of other states. I shall be able to stop any invasion, big or small.

HSIEH:　Big or small?

PRINCESS:　Yes! But of course you must give us your best wishes. Without your wishes there is no chance of victory. To

35　Your Majesty's health! *(She finds that her cup is empty.)* My maids!

Maids:　Yes, Your Highness!

PRINCESS:　More wine!

MAIDS *(serving):* Yes, Your Highness!

(Hsieh urges the Princess to drink more than she should and she gets drunk; she leans her head on the table.)

MAIDS: Her Highness has taken too much wine!

HSIEH *(pleased):* So she has! *(To himself.)* She has fallen   5
into my trap! *(To Attendants.)* Attendants!

ATTENDANTS: Yes, Your Majesty!

HSIEH: Help me to change my clothes.

ATTENDANTS: Yes, Your Majesty!

*(They all stand round him. He changes into the uniform of an   10
officer such as he was wearing in Act II.)*

HSIEH: Now I have done it. *(He takes a little yellow flag
from the Princess.)* With this yellow flag I can go where I like
and get away from the Western Regions. But I shall have to
leave without saying good-bye to the Princess.   15

FIRST ATTENDANT: Your Majesty, when you have gone, Her
Highness will ask about you. What shall we say to her?

HSIEH *(sitting down at the table again):* I will write a letter to
her. I can't bear to say good-bye to her. *(Reading as he writes.)*
'The New Year is coming and I am going to the border to in-   20
spect the soldiers there. If you still love me follow me, with all
your soldiers, to the Third Pass. If you don't love me stay where
you are and don't think of me.' *(To Attendants.)* Men of the
Western Regions, prepare my horse for me. When Her Highness
the Royal Princess wakes up, tell her that I have gone to the   25
border to inspect the soldiers there.

FIRST ATTENDANT: Yes, Your Majesty!

*(He gives Hsieh a whip. Hsieh mounts his horse and disap-
appears.)*

MAIDS: Your Highness! Your Highness!   30

PRINCESS *(waking up):* The wine has affected me a little.
(Looking round.) Where is His Majesty?

FIRST ATTENDANT: His Majesty has gone to the border to
inspect the troops there, Your Highness.

PRINCESS *(surprised):* Did he leave any orders for me?   35

FIRST ATTENDANT *(giving the letter to her):* His Majesty has
left this letter for Your Highness.

PRINCESS *(taking the letter)*: Let me read it. *(She reads the letter.)* What does he mean? What does he mean? *(She taps her fingers while walking about the stage.)* Ah, I see! His Majesty has gone back to China! He wants me to follow him with all the
5   soldiers to China! *(She calls.)* Attendants!

ATTENDANTS: Yes, Your Highness!

PRINCESS: Order my two officers Ma Ta and Kiang Hai, to wait for me before the palace gates with all my men.

ATTENDANTS: Yes, Your Highness!

10   FIRST ATTENDANT *(calls aloud)*: Her Highness the Royal Princess orders Ma Ta and Kiang Hai to wait for her before the palace gates with all her men!

VOICES *(off stage)*: To hear is to obey!

PRINCESS *(to herself)*: His Majesty is unkind. He should
15   not have gone away without saying good-bye. I will go and meet him and ask for the reason.

*(She goes off with the Attendants and Maids. Then four Soldiers, four Officers and Ma Ta and Kiang Hai appear. These two Officers have uniforms which make them look rather
20   stupid. They have funnily painted faces.)*

MA TA: Our home is far away in the north-west!

KIANG HAI: We usually do not know what to say!

MA TA: Beef and mutton are what we like best!

KIANG HAI: Big camels* are what we ride!

25   MA TA *(to the audience)*: I am Ma Ta, at your service!

KIANG HAI: I am Kiang Hai, your humble servant!

MA TA: I'm glad to see you.

KIANG HAI: How are you?

MA AND KIANG: We are here, waiting for orders from Her
30   Highness the Royal Princess.

(Four Flag-Bearers come running on to the stage. The Princess follows them with a spear and a whip which she keeps waving.)

PRINCESS: Oh, unfaithful Hsieh Ping-Kuei! I will catch up with you and punish you for not keeping your promise to marry
35   me.

*camel,   long-necked animal, with either one or two large lumps on its back.

MA AND KIANG: Our respects to you, Your Highness!

PRINCESS: Don't waste time. Are the men ready?

MA AND KIANG: Yes, Your Highness! We are waiting for your orders.

PRINCESS: Order them to march to the First Pass.   5

(They all go off in order. A small Pass is immediately built on the stage and its Guardian* appears with two soldiers.)

GUARDIAN: By the order of Her Highness the Royal Princess of the Western Regions I am the Guardian of the First Pass.

(Hsieh appears and calls aloud.)   10

HSIEH: Hey! Let me through the Pass!

GUARDIAN: Where do you come from and what is your business?

HSIEH: By the order of Her Highness the Royal Princess I have official business to do beyond the Pass.   15

GUARDIAN: Have you the yellow flag from Her Highness?

HSIEH: Yes, here it is. *(He shows him the flag.)*

GUARDIAN *(calls)*:   Soldiers, let this man through the Pass!

SOLDIERS: Yes, Your Honour!

(Hsieh goes through the small Pass. They have to raise it from   20
the ground to let Hsieh through without bending. As soon as he
has gone the Princess appears with her followers. The Guardian
kneels before her.)

GUARDIAN: The Guardian of the First Pass pays his respects to you, Your Highness!   25

PRINCESS: Don't stand on ceremony. Tell me quickly, has His Majesty the King passed here?

GUARDIAN *(trembling)*:   There was a man who passed through, but I don't know if it was His Majesty the King.

PRINCESS *(angry)*:   Don't you even know your King? You are   30
under arrest! *(She calls.)* To the Second Pass!

(They all go off. The same Pass is used as the Second Pass, and another Guardian appears with his men.)

SECOND GUARDIAN: By order of Her Highness the Royal

**Guardian,*   someone who looks after something, in this case,
            the Pass.

Princess of the Western Regions, I am the Guardian of the Second Pass.

(Hsieh appears again and calls aloud.)

HSIEH: Hey! Let me through the Second Pass!

5   SECOND GUARDIAN: Where do you come from and what is your business?

HSIEH: By the order of Her Highness the Royal Princess I have official business to do beyond the Pass.

SECOND GUARDIAN: Have you the yellow flag from Her
10   Highness?

HSIEH: Yes, here it is. *(He shows him the flag.)*

SECOND GUARDIAN *(calls):*   Soldiers, let this man through the Pass!

SOLDIERS: Yes, Your Honour!

15   *(Hsieh goes through it as before. The Princess arrives with her men and the Second Guardian kneels before her.)*

SECOND GUARDIAN: The Guardian of the Second Pass pays his respects to you, Your Highness!

PRINCESS: Don't stand on ceremony. I want to ask you
20   whether His Majesty the King has passed here?

SECOND GUARDIAN *(trembling):*   A man did pass here, but...

PRINCESS *(angry):*   You are useless! I shall have you arrested! *(She calls.)* To the Third Pass!

*(They all go off again. Though the Third Pass is in China, the
25   same Pass is used on stage. The only difference is that it is placed on the left instead of the right. The Guardian of this Chinese Pass, General Mu, is an old man. He appears, with four Soldiers walking in front of him.)*

MU: People know me by my white helmet,* white armour,
30   and white flags. I also have a white beard, and white eyebrows. After I have taken plenty of white wine I will show you the white of my eyes! I am Old Mu, the White General, at your service! By order of His Majesty the Emperor I am the Guardian of the Third Pass. *(He calls.)* Soldiers!

35   SOLDIERS: Yes, Your Honour!

MU: Lead the way to the tower of the Pass.

*helmet,   a head-cover for a soldier.

SOLDIERS: Yes, Your Honour!

(He sits on a chair placed on a table behind the Pass. Hsieh appears and speaks to himself first.)

HSIEH: I have now come to the borders of my own country: the Third Pass is the boundary. The man in the tower of the Pass looks like old General Mu. Let me call him by his name. *(He calls aloud.)* Hey! My respects to you, General Mu!

MU *(surprised)*: Thank you, thank you! Who are you and how do you know my name?

HSIEH: I am Captain Hsieh Ping-Kuei. I have come back from the Western Regions to report at army headquarters.*

MU *(frightened)*: But you were killed in the Western Regions. This must be your spirit which has come back!

HSIEH: No, I was not killed. My enemy tried to get me killed and thinks I am dead. But I am still alive.

MU: Is that so? I can hardly believe it.

(Shouting is heard.)

HSIEH: It's quite true. Oh, my dear old General, there are people coming after me. Please let me pass and we can talk later.

MU: All right. I don't think there is any danger if I let you in alone. Soldiers, let this man through the Pass!

SOLDIERS: Yes, Your Honour!

(The Pass is opened and Hsieh disappears through it. Meanwhile the Princess appears before the Pass with her soldiers.)

MA AND KIANG: Your Highness, we have now arrived at the Third Pass which belongs to China.

PRINCESS: So we have! Go and ask them to let us go through.

MA AND KIANG: Yes, Your Highness!

PRINCESS: Wait! One moment!

MA AND KIANG: Yes, Your Highness!

PRINCESS: Remember that we have come to another country. We must be more polite in our speech.

MA AND KIANG: Yes, Your Highness!

(Ma and Kiang face Old Mu.)

MA TA *(calling aloud)*: Hey, old man!

*headquarters,   in this case, the place from which an army is
                  controlled.

MU: Old moon? We can't see the old moon until midnight.

MA TA: My lord!

MU: He is in Heaven.

KIANG HAI: My Emperor!

5   MU: What are you two doing here? You are too ugly to be called human beings and certainly too ordinary to be called devils. The strangest thing about you is your legs: they are like those of an elephant. Go back and get someone better to talk to me!

MA AND KIANG *(to Princess):*   He wishes to speak to Your Highness.

PRINCESS: All right, I'll go. *(She goes forward.)* My respects to the old grandfather in the tower!

MU: Thank you, and mine to the little grandmother below.   5
What is your business here?

PRINCESS: I would like to ask you something. Has His Majesty the King of our country, Captain Hsieh Ping-Kuei of your country, passed through here?

MU: His Majesty the King of your country has not passed   10
but Captain Hsieh Ping-Kuei of our country has passed.

PRINCESS: Don't you know that Captain Hsieh Ping-Kuei of your country is no other than His Majesty the King of our country? If he is here, please ask him to appear on the wall of the Pass. I would like to say a few words to him. Then my soldiers and I will leave. There will be no trouble and no damage. Do you think this can be done, my old General?

MU: Captain Hsieh Ping-Kuei of our country used to be a strong young man. Now, after eighteen years in your country he has come back a weak old man. How can I allow him to see you again, you worthless creature?

PRINCESS *(angry)*: How dare you speak like that to me! *(Calls.)* Ma Ta! Kiang Hai!

MA AND KIANG: Yes, Your Highness!

PRINCESS: Attack the Pass!

MA AND KIANG: Yes, Your Highness!

(Drums are sounded and they all point their weapons at the Pass.)

MU *(frightened)*: Wait a moment! Wait a moment! *(They stop.)* The Pass is made of cloth; it will be damaged if you are not careful. You are a very wise and generous young lady. Don't be angry with an old fool like me. *(She laughs.)* If you will go back a little I will ask Captain Hsieh to come out and speak to you.

PRINCESS *(calling)*: I order the soldiers to retreat! *(They go off by the right entrance.)*

MU *(getting down from the tower)*: Captain Hsieh! Captain Hsieh!

HSIEH *(appearing from the left)*: Have you won a victory?

MU: The lady, my enemy, has won! The victory belongs to her. You are requested to go up to the tower; she wants to speak to you.

HSIEH: Thank you. *(He goes up to the tower; Mu leaves with the Soldiers.)* I see the Princess coming along.

PRINCESS *(appearing again)*: I see the unfaithful one standing alone. *(To Hsieh.)* What did I do to deserve this? Why did you run away from me?

HSIEH: I will tell you everything now. When I was at Court

the other day I heard a wild goose making sounds like those of a human voice. I shot it and found a letter written in blood from Lady Precious Stream.

PRINCESS: What! Who is Lady Precious Stream?

HSIEH: She is my wife!   5

PRINCESS: Your wife! So you are already married! Are you going back to her now?

HSIEH *(hanging down his head)*: Yes.

PRINCESS: So you have been deceiving me all these years!

HSIEH: No! You mustn't say that about me. I was in love   10
with you all the time and I still love you.

PRINCESS: Then why are you leaving me?

HSIEH: Because it is my duty to return to my wife.

PRINCESS: You should have told me this before.

HSIEH: I loved you very much and didn't want to hurt your   15
feelings.

PRINCESS: It is cruel of you to deceive me and then leave me. I will never speak to you again. I hate you! I hate you!

HSIEH *(hurt)*: Please don't hate me! I still love you. Why don't you be my sister and come to China with me?   20

PRINCESS: Never! Never! I don't want to be near you now.

HSIEH: But I want to be near you. That is why I asked you to follow me.

PRINCESS: Yes, but you won't marry me.

HSIEH: Don't say that. I would gladly marry you if I could.   25
Please, agree to be my sister and come with me.

PRINCESS: Never!

HSIEH *(not knowing how she feels)*: Then I must say good-bye for ever, because I may never see you again!

PRINCESS: I don't want to see you again!   30

HSIEH *(with feeling)*: Perhaps that's a very good thing. I don't think that you will be able to see me, even if you want to. I have many enemies in China and, without your protection, they will probably murder me very soon!

PRINCESS: Oh, I never thought of that! Yes, your General   35
Wei will try to murder you. I must go with you, to protect you, even though I hate you.

HSIEH *(pretending to refuse her help)* : No, I can't accept your protection if you still hate me. I have no wish to live if you hate me. I might as well be murdered.

PRINCESS : All right, I won't hate you.

5 HSIEH : And you will be my sister?

PRINCESS : No! Only your cousin.

HSIEH : No! Sister.

PRINCESS : Let us say first cousin?

HSIEH : No. Sister.

10 PRINCESS : All right. Come down at once.

HSIEH : No! Lady Precious Stream is in danger and I must hurry to her. Order your men to camp near the Pass. I will send a message very soon. Good-bye till then.

PRINCESS : Good-bye. *(He gets down and disappears. She*
15 *calls.)* Ma Ta! Kiang Hai! Order the soldiers to camp here.

MA AND KIANG *(coming with the Soldiers)* : Yes, Your Highness! *(They walk round the stage and go off. The Princess follows them.)*

VOICE *(shouting)* : 'Look out! A horse is coming!' *(Captain*
20 *Hsieh Ping-Kuei has arrived at a place quite near his home. He appears.)*

HSIEH : When a man is anxious to get home he travels both by day and by night. I have now arrived at the little hill not far from my own door. *(He gets off and ties his horse to a tree.)* Let
25 me tie my horse in the shade of a tree and ask those ladies about my wife. *(He calls aloud.)* My respects to you, ladies.

A VOICE *(off stage)* : The same to you, sir. Have you lost your way?

HSIEH : No, I'm not lost. I just want to inquire, madam,
30 about someone.

A VOICE *(off stage)* : To what family does the person belong?

HSIEH : She is the daughter of the Prime Minister Wang, and the wife of Hsieh Ping-Kuei.

A VOICE *(off stage)* : Oh, Precious Stream of the Wang fami-
35 ly! I'll call her for you, sir. *(She calls.)* My third sister, someone wants you.

PRECIOUS STREAM *(off stage)* : Thank you very much. I am

coming. *(She appears from the left with a little basket on her arm.)*
We have not see her for eighteen years but she does not look
very much older than the last time we saw her. Of course, she
has changed a lot. She has suffered much all these years but she
has managed to take care of her looks.)   5

HSIEH *(to himself)*:   There is someone coming. She looks like
my wife but I must make sure. I mustn't mistake another man's
wife for my own. Now that I have come home I must be very
polite. *(To her.)* My respects to you, madam. *(He puts his hands*
together and bows; she curtsies.)   10

PRECIOUS STREAM: And mine to you. Have you lost your
way, sir?

HSIEH: No! No one could be lost in a place like this! I want
to find someone.

PRECIOUS STREAM: Only famous people are known to me.   15

HSIEH: The one I'm looking for is a very famous person. She
is the daughter of the Prime Minister Wang, and the wife of
Hsieh Ping-Kuei. She is called Lady Precious Stream.

PRECIOUS STREAM: Are you a relative of hers, sir?

HSIEH: No, I am not.   20

PRECIOUS STREAM: Then an old friend?

HSIEH: No, not that, I'm afraid.

PRECIOUS STREAM: If you are neither her relative nor her
old friend, why are you asking for her?

HSIEH: Oh, there is a reason, madam! I am in the army,   25
together with her husband and he has given me a letter to her.
That is why I am asking for her, madam.

PRECIOUS STREAM: Precious Stream lives not far from here.
Please give that letter to me and I will deliver it to her for you,
sir.   30

HSIEH: My eldest brother, Hsieh Ping-Kuei, said that I must
give the letter to her myself.

PRECIOUS STREAM: What if you can't find her yourself?

HSIEH: Then I must take it back to him.

PRECIOUS STREAM: Please excuse me a moment.   35

HSIEH: Certainly.

PRECIOUS STREAM *(aside)*:   I should like to confess and get that letter at once, but I am in such rags that I am ashamed to do so. And if I don't he will certainly not give me that letter. Oh, how cruel that for eighteen long years we have never met, and have not been able even to write to each other! What shall I do? *(She taps her forehead with her fingers.)* Ah, I have an idea! *(To him.)* Well, sir, do you understand riddles?

HSIEH: A little.

PRECIOUS STREAM: Do you want to see Precious Stream?

HSIEH: Yes.

PRECIOUS STREAM: Now, if you look far...

HSIEH: She is a thousand miles away.

PRECIOUS STREAM: Yes, and if you look near...

HSIEH: She is before you! Then, am I speaking to Mrs. Hsieh, the famous daughter of the Prime Minister Wang?

PRECIOUS STREAM: Oh, no, not the famous, but only the humble wife of Hsieh Ping-Kuei.

HSIEH *(holding his hands together and bowing)*:   My respects to you.

PRECIOUS STREAM *(curtsies)*:   You have already paid your respects.

HSIEH: Over-politeness does no harm.

PRECIOUS STREAM *(smiling)*:   Well said. Now my husband's letter, please!

HSIEH: One moment. Will you excuse me a minute?

PRECIOUS STREAM: Certainly.

HSIEH *(aside)*:   Wait a moment. I was married to her only for a month and have been absent from home for eighteen years. I don't know what kind of woman she really is. Let me try to make love to her. If she proves to be a good and faithful woman I'll tell her who I am. If she proves to be unfaithful I'll go back to the Royal Princess of the Western Regions. I know that many great men have tested their own wives, so why shouldn't I? *(To her.)* Now, where have I put that letter?

PRECIOUS STREAM: Where is it?

HSIEH: It is lost, madam!

PRECIOUS STREAM *(anxiously)*:   How can it be lost? Where did you put it?

HSIEH: I put it in my arrow-holder, madam.

PRECIOUS STREAM: Isn't that a safe place?

HSIEH: Yes, it is, madam.

PRECIOUS STREAM: Then how could you have lost it?

HSIEH: Well, when I was not far from here, I happened to   5
take out an arrow to shoot at a wild goose...

PRECIOUS STREAM *(childishly):*   Why should you shoot a poor
wild goose?

HSIEH: I was hungry and wanted something to eat, madam.

PRECIOUS STREAM *(angry)*:   Yes, hungry! You are cruel!

HSIEH: Why should you be so upset about a letter?

PRECIOUS STREAM: Don't you know that a letter from one who loves you is worth all the money in the world? You should remember the saying: 'I examine myself three times every day to see whether I have done truly and loyally my best to my friend …' and you have lost the letter of your friend! *(She cries.)* I am heart-broken.

HSIEH: Don't take it so seriously, madam! If you are so anxious about that letter, I'll tell you something I remember that is in it.

PRECIOUS STREAM: Ah, I know what has happened! My husband sent some money with the letter. You have spent all the money on your way and destroyed the letter. So that is why you can remember something from it.

HSIEH: Don't say that, my dear madam! When my eldest brother, Hsieh Ping-Kuei, was writing the letter I happened to be beside him packing my things. So I looked over his shoulder and saw a few lines, madam.

PRECIOUS STREAM: Then your curiosity may prove useful.

HSIEH: Curious or not, I should not have lost the letter.

PRECIOUS STREAM: Please tell me what you can remember.

HSIEH: Listen carefully. 'On the mid-autumn night, under the bright moonlight…'

PRECIOUS STREAM: Stop! Don't you have lamps in your camps?

HSIEH: How can we have lamps there, madam? In camp all we have to depend on for light is the bright moonlight! 'Hsieh Ping-Kuei pays his respects to his dear wife…'

PRECIOUS STREAM: And mine to him. How has he been lately?

HSIEH: Very well.

PRECIOUS STREAM: Safe and sound?

HSIEH: Safe and sound.

PRECIOUS STREAM: How about his meals?

HSIEH: They were badly cooked by the soldiers.

PRECIOUS STREAM: How about his clothes?

HSIEH: He has had to wash and mend them himself!… 'And

begs to tell her that he has been very miserable lately. He has suffered a severe beating...'

PRECIOUS STREAM: He was beaten?

HSIEH: Yes, beaten, madam.

PRECIOUS STREAM: How many strokes did he receive?   *5*

HSIEH: Forty strokes in all.

PRECIOUS STREAM *(wiping away her tears)*:   Oh, my poor husband!

HSIEH: Don't cry, madam! There are still worse things coming! 'The other day a horse in his care was lost...'   *10*

PRECIOUS STREAM: Was it a government horse or was it privately owned?

HSIEH: How can there be any privately owned horses in a camp? Of course it was a government horse.

PRECIOUS STREAM: Then, I suppose he will have to pay for it?   *15*

HSIEH: Of course.

PRECIOUS STREAM: But where can he find the money to pay for it?

HSIEH: He is sure to be able to find it in some way or other. '... And because he had to pay for the horse he had to borrow   *20* ten pieces of silver.' *(Pointing to himself.)* Borrowed from me.

PRECIOUS STREAM: Stop! Allow me to ask you, what is your rank?

HSIEH: I am a captain.

PRECIOUS STREAM: And my husband, Hsieh Ping-Kuei's?   *25*

HSIEH: Also a captain.

PRECIOUS STREAM: If you are both captains you should get the same amount of pay. Then how could you lend him money while he had none?

HSIEH: There is a reason, madam. My eldest brother, Hsieh   *30* Ping-Kuei, spends all his pay. I, having been born in a humble family, have been used to saving all I get. In this way I was able to lend him the money to pay for the horse.

PRECIOUS STREAM: That is not true. My husband was also born in a humble family, and he wouldn't know how to spend   *35* his money even if he tried.

HSIEH *(laughing)*:   Ha, ha! This is the first time I have heard that he is also of humble birth.

PRECIOUS STREAM: Oh, dear, he is laughing at me!

HSIEH: With interest, he now owes me twenty pieces of silver and he has not paid me anything.

5   PRECIOUS STREAM: You ought to ask him to repay you.

HSIEH: It is difficult to get money from one who refuses to pay.

PRECIOUS STREAM: You should demand payment.

HSIEH: That would ruin our friendship.

10   PRECIOUS STREAM: What is that, hanging on your belt, sir?

HSIEH: My sword.

PRECIOUS STREAM: Then draw your sword if he refuses to pay.

HSIEH: The punishment for murder is death.

PRECIOUS STREAM: Then why mention the debt to me?

15   HSIEH: Because I want my money back, and it has something to do with you. *(She is surprised.)* I went to his camp to demand the money the other day, and he said that he had a wife at home, called Lady Precious Stream of the Wang family.

PRECIOUS STREAM: What! Let me ask you, has Precious
20   Stream ever owed you anything before?

HSIEH: No, nothing.

PRECIOUS STREAM: Has she borrowed anything from you recently?

HSIEH: No, nothing.

25   PRECIOUS STREAM: As she has neither borrowed from you before nor recently, why should her name be mentioned?

HSIEH: Well, let me ask you now, as the old saying goes: 'Father's debt…?'

PRECIOUS STREAM: 'The son pays.'

30   HSIEH: And 'The husband's debts…?'

PRECIOUS STREAM: 'The wife… the wife doesn't care anything for them!'

HSIEH: Well said! But still, the wife has to pay for them in some other way. Having no ready money, my eldest brother,
35   Hsieh, agreed to sell his wife; and you know, madam, he could get a buyer any time. So he immediately made a bargain with a certain officer.

PRECIOUS STREAM *(surprised)*: Ah! And who is this certain officer?

HSIEH *(with a smile)*: Do you understand riddles, madam?

PRECIOUS STREAM: A little.

HSIEH: Now, if you look far...   5

PRECIOUS STREAM: He is a thousand miles away.

HSIEH: Yes, and if you look near...

PRECIOUS STREAM: Do you mean that it is YOU?

HSIEH: Eh—eh—I have the proof!

PRECIOUS STREAM: What is your proof?   10

HSIEH: It is in the form of a marriage agreement.

PRECIOUS STREAM: Show it to me.

HSIEH *(hesitating)*: Yes—no! I am sure you are as virtuous as you are beautiful, and if once you have it in your hands you will tear it to pieces. What could I do then? I should lose both   15
my money and my wife.

PRECIOUS STREAM: What are you going to do?

HSIEH: I would like you to go with me to someone's house not far from here. Then let us invite some old men to come and see that I have the agreement.   20

PRECIOUS STREAM: Then it is really true that there is such an agreement?

HSIEH: Why should I lie to you?

PRECIOUS STREAM: Oh, cruel! *(On second thoughts.)* No, I still can't believe it. Who signed this agreement?   25

HSIEH: They are—they are Su, the Dragon General, Wei, the Tiger General, and Wang Yun, the Prime Minister!

PRECIOUS STREAM: Nonsense! I won't believe it now. Because they are all my near relatives, and they would certainly not allow my husband to sell me! Let us go to them and prove your   30
agreement is false.

HSIEH: No, I won't go to them, because they hate me, and they certainly won't side with me.

PRECIOUS STREAM: Ha! Then you know my relatives! Though *I* am poor my father is rich. Let us see how much my husband   35
owes you altogether and my father will send the money to you, even if you are far away in the Western Regions. Don't wait for

me now. I'll say good-bye, and you can wait for the money in the Western Regions. *(She turns to go back.)*

HSIEH *(stopping her):*   No, no! It took me forty-eight days to travel from the Western Regions to here, and I have come here
5   especially, not for the money but for you!

PRECIOUS STREAM *(frightened):*   If you go on speaking non-sense and insulting me I'll call for help and have you arrested! Then you will be sorry.

HSIEH: If you prefer our case to be dealt with by the law you
10   are as good as my wife.

PRECIOUS STREAM: How dare you!

HSIEH *(going nearer to her):*   If you really are such a virtuous woman as you pretend to be you ought to stay in your home. Why do you stand in a public place and talk with a stranger.
15   I love you; I am going to carry you off to the Western Regions!

PRECIOUS STREAM *(aside):*   Oh! I am frightened! The man is a beast without any manners. What shall I do? There is no help near here! Let me think. *(She taps her forehead with her fingers.)* Ah, I have it! I'll blind him! *(To him.)* Hallo, sir, some-
20   one is coming over there.

HSIEH *(turning away):*   Where?

PRECIOUS STREAM *(picking up a handful of imaginary sand, she throws it at him and runs away):*   Good-bye!

HSIEH *(a very happy man):*   Ha, ha, ha! A virtuous woman
25   indeed. No use trying to catch her. It's not very far, so I will not ride, but walk to my cave to meet her.

(He takes the whip and leads his horse away to the left, Precious Stream immediately comes from the right. The audience are now expected to imagine the cave before them.)

30   PRECIOUS STREAM *(running round the front of stage):*   Oh, no! He's following me!

HSIEH *(appearing and following her):*   I am your husband, Hsieh Ping-Kuei!

PRECIOUS STREAM *(entering the cave and closing the door):*
35   Let me shut the door and lock it. *(She shows this by placing a chair with its back to the audience.)*

HSIEH *(dropping the whip and knocking at the back of the chair):*

Open the door; you are shutting out your own husband.

PRECIOUS STREAM: You said a short time ago that you were an officer who knew my husband. Now you say you are my husband! You must be mad!

HSIEH: Oh, no! Let me prove to you that I am your husband. Don't you remember that you helped me with money and told me to be present on the second day of February, when I caught the embroidered ball? We were driven out by your father and lived in this cave. Then I shot and killed the man-eating tiger, and was made a captain and joined the Western Army. I was ordered to leave at once. I came back to tell you the news. I couldn't bear to leave you alone and you were equally sorry for me to go. There was little time and I had to ride off while you were not looking. And that was eighteen years ago.

PRECIOUS STREAM *(wiping her tears):*   Did you receive my letter?

HSIEH: Oh, yes! I received it only a short time ago. That is why I hurried home. If you don't believe me, here is that very letter.

PRECIOUS STREAM *(opening the door a little):*   Let me look at it. *(Closing the door again.)* No! How can you be my husband with such a long beard?

HSIEH: Why not?

PRECIOUS STREAM: My husband is a good-looking young man!

HSIEH: Thank you, third sister! But you ought to say he used to be good-looking and young. Don't you think that eighteen long and difficult years in the Western Regions would make him look rather old? If his beard were to grow only an inch a year it would become very long in eighteen years. *(Stroking his beard with his hands.)* Take yourself, for instance, my third sister. You are quite different from the young girl who threw the embroidered ball. Look in a looking-glass and tell me what you think.

PRECIOUS STREAM: Don't you know that there is no looking-glass in the humble cave?

HSIEH: Oh, I forgot! Look into a basin of water, as you always did before.

PRECIOUS STREAM: It is a long time since I looked into a basin of water, because I did not care how I looked. *(She looks into an imaginary basin.)* Oh, horrible! I am terribly aged! I couldn't call myself Precious Stream now if I met myself in the street!

HSIEH: But I do. Now open the door and let me in.

PRECIOUS STREAM *(opening the door a little and stretching out a hand):* Show me the letter first.

HSIEH *(giving her the letter, which she takes):* Here you are, my third sister.

PRECIOUS STREAM *(closing the door again):* Yes, this is the letter.

HSIEH: Then why do you close the door again?

PRECIOUS STREAM: I will open the door only on one condition.

HSIEH: What is your condition, please?

PRECIOUS STREAM: A very simple one. I only want you to go backward one step.

HSIEH *(doing so):* All right, I have done so.

PRECIOUS STREAM: Another step, please.

HSIEH *(doing so):* All right. Now open the door.

PRECIOUS STREAM: One step more, please.

HSIEH *(finding himself standing at the very edge of the stage):* No, I can't. I have come to the end of things.

PRECIOUS STREAM *(bitterly):* If you had not come to the end of things I am sure you would never have come back to me!

HSIEH: Oh, nonsense!

PRECIOUS STREAM: And after having left me for eighteen years you insulted me the moment you met me! What is there to live for? I'd rather die than go back to such a husband!

HSIEH: Please don't say that! I beg you to forgive me!

PRECIOUS STREAM: No!

HSIEH: I beg you on my knees! *(He kneels on one knee.)* Look! I am paying you my highest respects in the presence of thousands!

PRECIOUS STREAM *(looking through the bars on the back of the chairs, just as a Western lady would look through a keyhole on such an occasion)*: No, I won't look at you! But how about your other knee? I thought you said you were on your knees!

HSIEH: Oh, I beg your pardon! *(His other knee is on the ground now.)*

PRECIOUS STREAM: Ah! that's better! *(She opens the door by removing the chair first.)* Come in, my dear! *(She helps him up.)*

HSIEH *(getting up and going in)*: Thank you, my dear! *(He sits on a chair provided for him.)*

PRECIOUS STREAM *(sitting down too)*: To what rank have you risen after these eighteen years?

HSIEH *(his pride hurt)*: Eh? When your husband has returned from thousands of miles away, the first question you ask him is not about his health or whether he needs food or drink, but about his rank! What is rank compared with food and drink? Can you eat and drink it?

PRECIOUS STREAM: As you have not said a word about food and drink, I thought you were not interested in such things. Besides, I have not always had enough food and drink during these eighteen years, so I am likely to forget them.

HSIEH: What do you mean? Do you mean to tell me that you haven't had enough to eat and drink during my absence? I remember sending you the things you needed just before I left.

PRECIOUS STREAM: What was it?

HSIEH: Half a ton of firewood and a quarter of a ton of rice.

PRECIOUS STREAM *(imitating him)*: 'Half a ton of firewood and a quarter of a ton of rice.' Do you think these could have lasted for eighteen years?

HSIEH: I suppose not! But you ought to have gone to your father and brother-in-law, Wei, for further supplies.

PRECIOUS STREAM: They said that your pay had been stopped and they offered to lend me money, which I refused.

HSIEH: Excellent! Good-bye! *(He prepares to go.)*

PRECIOUS STREAM: Where are you gong?

HSIEH: To His Excellency the Prime Minister's house!

PRECIOUS STREAM *(catching his arm and leading him back to his chair)*: Don't go. My father is not very well.

HSIEH: What is the matter with him?

PRECIOUS STREAM: The common sickness of great men who don't like to see their relatives!

HSIEH: It doesn't matter. I haven't that kind of sickness, and I will agree to see him!

5   PRECIOUS STREAM: What are you talking about? *You* agree to see His Excellency the Prime Minister!

HSIEH: Yes, we have to sometimes.

PRECIOUS STREAM: What do you mean?

HSIEH *(very lightly):* He is so old and bad-tempered. If he
10   should offer to drive my horse, I would not have him.

PRECIOUS STREAM *(smiling):* Please don't talk as if you were dreaming. Wake up, my dear!

HSIEH: I am a practical man and was never a dreamer. Every word of what I say is true.

15   PRECIOUS STREAM: Are you saying that His Excellency the Prime Minister is willing to offer to drive your horse? Non-sense! The King is the only man in the world whom he serves.

HSIEH: Yes, that is quite true. But I have not said that I am not a king.

20   PRECIOUS STREAM *(nearly out of her senses):* You a king!

HSIEH: Yes. Only the King of the Western Regions, and I regret to say that I have not a very large country.

PRECIOUS STREAM *(hardly believing her ears):* Only the King of the Western Regions! I can't believe it! What proof have you?

25   HSIEH: What proof do you want?

PRECIOUS STREAM: Show me your royal seal.*

HSIEH: Nonsense! People do not ask a king to prove himself as a king by showing his royal seal.

PRECIOUS STREAM: But I have heard and seen that done
30   many times.

HSIEH: Have you? Where was it done, and who did it?

PRECIOUS STREAM *(childishly):* On the stage, done by the players!

HSIEH: Oh, but we are not on the stage and we are not
35   players!

---

*seal,   a small, decorated piece of metal, wood, etc., which is used to stamp a special mark on letters, etc.

PRECIOUS STREAM: It has been said: 'The world is a stage, human beings are only players, and life is a poor, sad play!' Besides, I have never seen a royal seal, and I want very much to see one. Do show it to me!

HSIEH: All right. If I have the royal seal...   *5*

PRECIOUS STREAM: Show it to me and I will believe you are a king.

HSIEH: Then let me arrange my hat properly and dust my jacket first. *(He produces the royal seal.)* Here is the seal of the King of the Western Regions.   *10*

PRECIOUS STREAM *(taking it with both hands, and after examining it carefully handing it back to Hsieh)*:   Oh, indeed, the royal seal of the King of the Western Regions! I must now kneel down before Your Majesty to pay my respects. *(She kneels down.)*   *15*

HSIEH *(speaking like a king)*:   Who is she that kneels before me?

PRECIOUS STREAM *(humbly)*:   She is Your Majesty's humble maid, Precious Stream of the Wang family.

HSIEH: And why have you come?   *20*

PRECIOUS STREAM: To pay my respects to Your Majesty.

HSIEH: You were very rude to me when you addressed me on the spot not far from the cave.

PRECIOUS STREAM: Your humble maid did not know it was Your Majesty.   *25*

HSIEH *(pleased)*:   If you had known then, would you have been more polite?

PRECIOUS STREAM: Had she known then, she would have been more impolite!

HSIEH *(surprised)*:   Indeed! Then I give you nothing at all.   *30* There is nothing more to say.

PRECIOUS STREAM *(prepared for the worst)*:   Then now she must use the most impolite words.

HSIEH *(covering his ears with both hands)*:   Do not say any more. I am about to give you a high honour. Hear me.   *35*

PRECIOUS STREAM *(feeling happy)*:   Yes, Your Majesty!

HSIEH: By the order of His Majesty the King of the Western

Regions, Lady Precious Stream of the Wang family is to be crowned Her Majesty the Queen of the Western Regions!

PRECIOUS STREAM: I thank you, Your Majesty! At last!

HSIEH *(helping her to get up):*   I have not taken care of
5   you these eighteen years.

PRECIOUS STREAM: And I have been thinking of you all the time.

HSIEH: Aren't you glad that we are at last united?

PRECIOUS STREAM: Yes. But I am afraid it is only a dream.
10   Please pinch* me to make sure.

HSIEH: Nonsense! Can't you see the bright sun there? You are not dreaming. I couldn't bear to pinch you.

PRECIOUS STREAM: Then I must pinch you. *(She pinches him.)*

HSIEH: Ouch! Ouch! You are mad!

PRECIOUS STREAM *(smiling)*:   Then I am not dreaming. I am   5 not dreaming.

HSIEH: Shall we go, my Queen?

(They leave.)

---

*to pinch,   to pull between the finger and the thumb.

Act IV

Early the next morning, we once more have the honour of waiting upon His Excellency the Prime Minister, Wang, at his house. It happens to be his sixtieth birthday.

The peaceful garden, we find, after eighteen years' absence, is
5 *not altered in any way. The huge rock still remains in the centre as no one has been able to move it back to its place at the side.*

Two Attendants enter, followed by His Excellency the Prime Minister, Wang.

WANG: To be Prime Minister is to be second to none and
10 above all other officers! *(He is helped to sit down.)* To most people my post seems a very happy one, but I have had more than enough of it. I regard it as scarcely worth all the trouble it gives. If you are unpopular everyone blames you and if you are popular you receive endless good wishes, which is even worse!
15 A famous politician is like a famous actor, everybody wants to pat him on the back! And you need at least a dozen secretaries to pick out the letters of your real friends from the thousands of others from people you don't know. The worst time of all is your birthday. Once a year you must let thousands of people
20 send you good wishes on a matter which was no doing of yours! If there is another ceremony I shall go mad!

A VOICE *(off stage)*: Lady Precious Stream comes to pay her respects to His Excellency her father and Madam her mother!

FIRST ATTENDANT *(kneeling before Wang)*: I beg to report,
25 Your Excellency, that Lady Precious Stream has come to pay her respects to His Excellency!

WANG *(surprised)*: What! Tell the maids to bring her in. *(He wipes his face.)*

FIRST ATTENDANT: Yes, Your Excellency! *(Calling out.)*
30 Show Lady Precious Stream in, please.

A VOICE *(off stage)*: You are requested to go in, Lady Precious Stream.

PRECIOUS STREAM *(off stage)*: I am coming, thank you!

(Two Maidservants lead her to the front of the stage. She is still plainly dressed, with no decoration on her head, and no jewels. She seems to be an entirely different woman, happy, cheerful and above all, sure of herself.)

PRECIOUS STREAM: Having said good-bye to my husband at our cave, I now come here to carry out what he has told me to do. Yesterday we met for the first time after eighteen years of separation. He told me that I ought to go to the Prime Minister's house to collect all the pay due to him. Years and years have passed since I was last at the Prime Minister's house, which is now newly painted and beautifully decorated, and quite different from what it used to be! Well, here is the garden at last.

FIRST MAID: Your humble maids present their respects to you, and bid you welcome, Lady Precious Stream.

PRECIOUS STREAM: Thank you! How is my dear mother, and has my father returned from Court?

FIRST MAID: Madam has not been very well lately because she has been worrying about you too much. His Excellency has just returned from Court.

PRECIOUS STREAM: Oh, my poor, dear mother! I should have been here long, long ago but I said that I would not return unless we were rich or successful. Even now I would not want to see my father if my husband had not sent me. Please let me in, my maids.

MAIDS: Yes, Lady Precious Stream.

(They turn and enter the garden.)

PRECIOUS STREAM *(kneeling before her father)*: Your daughter, Precious Stream, presents her respects to her father.

WANG *(unable to believe that this is his daughter)*: You, Precious Stream?

PRECIOUS STREAM: Yes, Your Excellency!

WANG *(with feeling)*: Oh, my dear daughter!

PRECIOUS STREAM *(moved)*: Oh, my dear Father!

WANG *(controlling his feelings)*: Don't stand on ceremony, my child. *(Aside.)* Not having seen her for eighteen years I can't stop the tears from coming to my eyes the moment we meet! *(He wipes his tears.)* I wonder what brought her to my house. *(To her.)* Take a seat.

5   PRECIOUS STREAM *(sitting down on a chair)*:   Thank you. How have you been lately, Father?

WANG: I have been very well. Now, my child, what has brought you here?

PRECIOUS STREAM: To wish you well on your birthday, dear
10 Father!

WANG *(finding the subject not to his liking)*:   Oh, nonsense! Why should you remember my birthday when you had no wish to remember me?

PRECIOUS STREAM *(coldly)*:   There are things which one can-
15 not forget even if one tries!

WANG: Yes! Yes! No! No! *(Feeling very uncomfortable.)* Go to the inner room to see your mother.

PRECIOUS STREAM: Yes! Your orders will be obeyed! *(She feels hurt and says to herself.)* My father is still annoyed with me
20 and does not wish to speak to me. I now go to the inner room to see my dear mother.

(She and the Maids go out. A Servant enters again.)

SERVANT *(kneeling before Wang)*:   I beg to report to Your Excellency that your two sons-in-law, the great Dragon General
25 and the great Tiger General, have come to wish you well on your birthday.

WANG: Show them here.

SERVANT *(going)*:   Yes, Your Excellency!

*(Su, the Dragon General, and Wei, the Tiger General, appear
30 in beautiful gowns. They look much the same as before but we can tell by the length of their beards that many years have passed since we last saw them. They are welcomed by music. They greet their father-in-law by holding their hands together and bowing. Their greeting is returned and seats are given to them. The music
35 stops.)*

SU AND WEI: How are you, my dear Father-in-law?

WANG: As usual, thank you. Now, my two excellent sons-in-law, don't tell me that you have come to wish me well on my birthday.

SU AND WEI: That is exactly what we have come for.

WANG: My heavens! Now let us talk about something else. Do you know that we have a rare visitor here today?

SU AND WEI: No, dear Father-in-law.

WANG: And this is the great difference between this and the past years. We have reason to be happy.

SU AND WEI: Why?

WANG: My third daughter has come back to me at last!

SU AND WEI *(surprised)*:   Who?

WANG: Precious Stream, my third daughter! Don't you know her?

SU AND WEI: Oh, yes! Of course!

WANG: She has come back at last.

WEI: Ha, ha! Now, old Su, I feel sure that our third sister-in-law is tired of her lonely life in her cave and has come back to find a second husband. We live and learn.

SU: We live, it is true, but learn nothing. After so many years, can't you see now that she is very determined and brave and would rather die then give in? She said that she would never come back to her father's house unless she was rich and success-ful.

WEI: But she is not rich, as we all know. And today she has come.

SU: She wouldn't come without good reason.

WEI: To marry again is a very good reason.

WANG: Well, my excellent sons-in-law, I also want her to marry again. During the feast I will try my best to persuade her to do so; and if I fail, I want you two to help me.

SU: I will try, but I am afraid...

WEI: Of course we will. You can depend upon us.

WANG: Thank you! *(He calls.)* Attendants!

ATTENDANT: Yes, Your Excellency!

WANG: Tell the maidservant to request Madam and the three young ladies to come here.

ATTENDANT: Yes, Your Excellency!

(One of the Attendants calls, and a female voice off stage answ-
wers. Then the voices of Madam and the three Young Ladies are
heard saying that they are coming. They immediately appear in
beautiful dresses, with two Maids walking in front of them.
Again there is music. They are welcomed by everyone and seats
are provided for them. They drink while the music is playing, and
speak only when it stops.)

WANG: Serve the wine at once.

(Music.)

ATTENDANT: The feast is ready, Your Excellency.

(Music.)

WANG *(raising his cup):*   Drink, my dear sons-in-law.

SU AND WEI: Thank you, dear Father-in-law.

(Music.)

ALL: We wish you good health, Father!

(Music.)

WANG: Now, Precious Stream!

PRECIOUS STREAM: Yes, Your Excellency!

WANG: My dear daughter!

PRECIOUS STREAM: My dear Father!

WANG: I have something to say to you, but I don't know
whether I ought to say it during this feast.

PRECIOUS STREAM: A father's advice to his daughter is welcome at any time.

WANG: As your husband died in the Western Regions years
ago, I, being your father, am worried about you. I should like to
choose a suitable husband for you. As I am getting old, I wish
to have a son-in-law to live with me. What do you think of that
my child?

PRECIOUS STREAM: Oh, no, Father, I don't believe my husband is dead and, even if he were, I would remain a widow and
be faithful to his memory.

WANG: My dear child, you know nothing about life! The
saying goes: 'To remain a widow and be faithful to your husband's memory is easily said but difficult to carry out to the end.
If you can't carry out your words loyally to the end you will
be laughed at by everyone!'

PRECIOUS STREAM: I think the saying is: 'To remain a widow and be faithful to your husband's memory is easily said but difficult to carry out to the end. If you can't carry it out to the end, that is none of your father's business!'

WANG *(angry):*   Silence! I would rather see you dead than   5
hear everybody laugh at you!

MADAM: While you are scolding my Precious Stream you are breaking her heart!

GOLDEN STREAM: And mine, too!

WANG *(turning angrily to her):*   What is she to you? She pre-   10
ferred to leave you and live in a cave!

MADAM: So? She may be poor but she is honest. Did she ever take anything from the Prime Minister's house?

GOLDEN STREAM: No! I know she did not.

WANG: She was entirely spoiled by you!   15

(He turns away and takes no notice of his wife.)

MADAM *(turning away from him too):*   Now, my child, don't mind what your father says to you. Just do as you think best and you will have all my good wishes.

GOLDEN STREAM: And mine too.   20

PRECIOUS STREAM *(not wishing her mother and father to quarrel):*   Here are my respects to you, dear Father and Mother. *(She curtsies.)* and I beg your permission to say a few words to you.

WANG: Let us hear them.   25

PRECIOUS STREAM: I, the most unfortunate of your daughters, was not born to have a good husband, so please don't try to change things for me. The death of my husband, Hsieh Ping-Kuei, in the Western Regions, is but a story, and I myself don't believe it in the least. Even if it proved to be true, you ought to   30
discuss the matter privately with no other person present but we three: father, mother and daughter. Now here we have the two gentlemen, my brothers-in-law...

WEI: No, my dear sister-in-law, we are close relatives by marriage.   35

PRECIOUS STREAM: Yes, you are the close relative who wants to kill us!

WANG: Don't say that! I am sure he was sorry about your husband's death and has been trying to help you! *(To Wei and Su.)* Now, my excellent sons-in-law, will you try and say something to her for me?

SU *(rising):* Yes, dear Father-in-law. Allow me to try first, Wei.

GOLDEN STREAM: Use only kind words, dear.

WEI: Try your best, old Su!

SU: Of course. *(He goes to Precious Stream.)* My dear sister-in-law, here are my respects to you.

PRECIOUS STREAM *(with a curtsy):* Thank you, and here are mine to you, my dear brother-in-law.

SU: Thank you! I have a few words to say to you, and I hope you will have patience and hear them to the end. The report of the death of my brother-in-law, Hsieh Ping-Kuei, is without proof, and you need not be bothered about the advice of your father to marry again. Nobody can make you marry again unless you yourself are willing to do so.

PRECIOUS STREAM: Thank you, my dear brother-in-law! I also have a few private words to say to you. We have to thank you for the kind help you gave to my husband when he was on his Western Expedition.* We have discovered who caused the trouble. Yesterday a certain person came back...

SU: Who is this certain person?

PRECIOUS STREAM: A man by the name of Hsieh!

SU: Oh!

PRECIOUS STREAM: Not a word. It is still a secret. If anyone asks you about him you must pretend that you know nothing.

SU *(smiling):* All right. I promise. *(To himself.)* Precious Stream is indeed a wonderful woman! *(Going to Wei.)* Now, Wei, I am not able to do anything, but I hope you will have better luck.

WEI *(rising):* Old Su, you are indeed a good-for-nothing old fool! How can a great big man like you fail to persuade a woman! Let me go to her, and before I have said half a dozen words she is sure to agree to marry again.

SU: Very well. *(He sits.)*

*expedition, in this case, a journey made by an army.

GOLDEN STREAM: Let us see what you can do.

WEI *(to himself)*: I'll try my best to be friendly, and give her one of my charming smiles. *(He smiles charmingly and addresses Precious Stream.)* My dear sister-in-law, your father's suggestion that you should marry again is for your own good. I would like you to consider it carefully. *(Receiving no answer, he speaks louder.)* For your own good, my dear sister-in-law.

PRECIOUS STREAM *(looking away from him)*: Who is the man rocking backwards and forwards in front of me?

WEI *(surprised)*: Why? Don't you recognize my musical voice and know that I am your brother-in-law, Wei?

PRECIOUS STREAM: Are you trying to say that you are Wei, the Tiger General?

WEI: Yes, your brother-in-law, Wei, the famous Tiger General!

PRECIOUS STREAM: What is your business here?

WEI: Eh—eh—

PRECIOUS STREAM: Are you trying to persuade me to marry again?

WEI *(awkwardly)*: Ah? Yes! Life for a widow is unbearable.

PRECIOUS STREAM: What you are saying is…

WEI *(continuing her sentence)*: Quite right.

PRECIOUS STREAM: Just nonsense! How dare you speak of such a thing to me! The day you are under my control you shall pay for this!

WEI: What you are saying is just nonsense, too! How can I ever be under your control? Even if I were, I would not care! Nonsense! All this is nonsense!

PRECIOUS STREAM: All right. We shall see about it.

(Wei goes to his seat angrily and Silver Stream walks over to her sister.)

SILVER STREAM: Excuse me for a minute, please.

WEI: Where are you going?

SILVER STREAM: To try to persuade my sister to remarry.

WEI: You had better not. I have failed to persuade her.

SILVER STREAM: But I am different, for I am her sister. I will succeed.

WEI: If she consents to remarry, don't let her marry anyone else...

SILVER STREAM: Whom do you propose she should marry?

WEI: Eh—eh—you, I and she would be very happy
5   together.

SILVER STREAM: What you are saying is...

WEI: Quite right.

SILVER STREAM: Nonsense! *(Wei sinks to his seat and she addresses her sister.)* My dear sister, here are my respects to you,
10   and I hope you will listen to your older sister and to reason.
Everybody says that Hsieh Ping-Kuei is dead, so why don't you
believe it and marry someone who will make your life happy at
last? Do follow the advice of your elders and you will be happy.

PRECIOUS STREAM *(to her sister)*:   You think you are wise and
15   pretty, rich and happy, do you? Will you come with me to have
a look at your unfortunate husband? He is the picture of dis-
honesty! Look at his big nose! Look at his eyes, they stick out
like a pair of teacups! And what an enormous stomach he has!
Anyone who has married such an object is not qualified to give
20   me advice on marriage. My husband is at least better than that,
even if I don't regard him as perfect!

SILVER STREAM *(quarrelling with her sister)*:   Pooh! What to
you seems to be ugliness is, to me, real beauty! I think my
husband is the finest man who ever lived! And pray what
25   can you say about your beggar-husband, Hsieh Ping-Kuei, who
can hardly ever get a penny by begging? *(She sits again, quite
angry.)*

PRECIOUS STREAM: To be a cheat is worse than to be an
honest beggar! Wei, your husband, has been cheating me all
30   these eighteen years out of my husband's pay!

SILVER STREAM: What do you mean?

WEI: How dare you say that I have been cheating!

SILVER STREAM: How dare you!

PRECIOUS STREAM: You should give me my husband's pay.

35   WEI: Dead men receive no pay. If he is alive I am quite ready
to pay what is due to him.

PRECIOUS STREAM: If my husband Hsieh Ping-Kuei is alive,

you will pay?

WEI *(who is sure that Hsieh is dead)*:   Not only pay him what is due but double the amount!

PRECIOUS STREAM: You will keep your promise?

WEI: Certainly!   5

SILVER STREAM: My husband always keeps his promises.

PRECIOUS STREAM *(to all)*:   I want you, dear Father and Mother, and you, my sisters and my other brother-in-law, to be the witnesses. If my husband Hsieh Ping-Kuei is alive, he, Wei, the Tiger General, will pay double the amount due to him.   10

WEI: Yes, if he is alive.

PRECIOUS STREAM *(getting up and going away)*:   Excuse me a few minutes. *(To herself.)* I must leave the Prime Minister's house and bring my husband here from the cave.

(She leaves.)   15

WANG *(feeling uncomfortable)*:   Precious Stream seems to be very sure of herself today. It may be true that her husband Hsieh Ping-Kuei *is* still alive!

SU: Yes, I think he is. I think he is.

GOLDEN STREAM: And I think so too.   20

WEI: No! Rubbish! It was I, with my own eyes, who saw him pulled down from his horse by the foreign princess in the Western Regions and cut into three pieces by her. And in the wild excitement I stamped my right foot three times on his dead body like this. *(He stamps three times.)*   25

SILVER STREAM: Well done, dear!

SU: Why did you do that?

GOLDEN STREAM: Yes, why did you do that?

WEI: It was to make sure that he could never come to life again!   30

SU: Nonsense!

GOLDEN STREAM: Nonsense!

WANG: It would be a good thing to have him dead.

MADAM: No, it would be better to have him alive.

WEI AND SILVER STREAM: Better to have him dead.   35

SU AND GOLDEN STREAM: No, better to have him alive.

VOICES *(off stage)*:   We are coming.

(Precious Stream returns victoriously with her husband, Hsieh Ping-Kuei, who is still dressed as an officer. They come to the front of the stage.)

PRECIOUS STREAM *(pulling her husband forward a few steps)*:
5   My dear husband, we are going to His Excellency the Prime Minister's house to pay a visit. You must wear your hat straight. *(She puts his hat straight.)* Look at the dust on your clothes. *(she dusts his clothes.)* and the dirt on your face! *(She taps his face lightly whilst he moves it away.)* You don't look at all a fit
10   person to pay such an important visit!

HSIEH: Behave yourself!

PRECIOUS STREAM: No, the saying goes: 'The official depends on his seal, the tiger on the mountain cave, and the wife on her good husband.' I have had no one to depend on for eighteen
15   years. Now that you have come back I have someone to depend on, and I must do often now what I was unable to do before.

HSIEH: Oh, you are troublesome!

PRECIOUS STREAM: Every woman who has a husband must be

troublesome. Heaven made me like this so I can't help it.

HSIEH: Let us go to see your father and mother and end your joking. *(They turn and enter the garden.)*

WEI *(dreamily)*: Better to have him dead!

HSIEH: Ah, there is my enemy! *(He stands still, looking as   5
if he could kill Wei.)*

PRECIOUS STREAM *(cheerfully)*: Now, my dear husband, why don't you take a seat?

HSIEH: In such grand surroundings as these how can we two dare to sit down?   10

PRECIOUS STREAM: As everyone else is allowed to sit down I think we should also have our seats. You step aside and let me bring a chair for you. *(She goes calmly to bring a chair.)*

HSIEH: I am afraid that if we do sit down it will make trouble.

PRECIOUS STREAM *(carrying a chair raised over her head, puts   15
it noisily on the floor)*: Never mind. If there is any trouble you have your wife to protect you, my dear! *(She pushes him into the chair next to hers.)*

HSIEH: Thank you, my dear! Under the protection of my wife, I, Hsieh Ping-Kuei, sit down!

(The situation seems to be very awkward. Wang coughs uneasily and tries to attract the attention of Precious Stream, but she takes no notice of him.)

WANG: Ahem! Ahem! Well, Precious Stream!

PRECIOUS STREAM *(not looking at him)*:   Ahem!

WANG: Eh? Who—who is the man sitting there?

PRECIOUS STREAM: So you have seen him at last! He is no other than the person who refused to die in the Western Regions. He has now come back to get his revenge.

WANG *(feeling more uncomfortable and addressing Su)*:   Will you kindly go and see who he is?

SU: Certainly.

WANG: Thank you.

WEI: Where are you going, old Su?

SU: To see whether it is really Hsieh Ping-Kuei who has come back.

WEI: You will have bad luck after this because he is really dead and you can only see his spirit.

SU *(going to Hsieh)*:   Are you my brother-in-law, Hsieh Ping-Kuei? How do you do?

HSIEH: How do you do, my dear Su, the great Dragon General?

SU: When did you come back? Please excuse me for offering you my welcome so late!

HSIEH: Please don't stand on ceremony. And I hope you will excuse me if I have not returned my thanks to you before. I owe you much for having saved my life in the Western Regions.

SU: Don't mention that. Have you some special business here?

HSIEH: Yes, I want to settle an old account with somebody here.

SU *(trying to smooth the matter over)*:   Come and join the feast first, and we can discuss it over a cup of wine.

HSIEH: No, thank you! I will not sit at the same table with my enemy. Don't worry about me, please.

SU: Then I will see you later. *(He goes back to his seat.)* I beg to report to Your Excellency that it really is my brother-in-law who has come back.

GOLDEN STREAM: I knew he would come back!

WEI *(interrupting her):*   Nonsense! I am sure you will die very   5
soon because you must have seen his spirit. He is dead.

SU *(not wishing to argue with him):*   Go and look for yourself.

WEI: I will, of course. He is dead; how can he come back in the flesh? *(Sees Hsieh.)* Ah! It is Hsieh Ping-Kuei! I have been try-   10
ing my best to kill him and now how can I face him? *(He taps his forehead with his fingers.)* Ah! I have it! The old saying goes: 'All ugliness is hidden by a smile!' Let me greet him with a smile. I think then he will forget the wrong I have done him. *(He makes faces and then turns to Hsieh.)* Oh, so this is you, my dear brother-   15
in-law, Hsieh Ping-Kuei! Ha! ha! ha! ha! ha! *(He holds his hands together and bows.)* Welcome home! When did you return? *(To himself.)* Ah! he seems to be deaf! Let me try again *(To Hsieh.)* So this is you, my dear brother-in-law, Hsieh Ping-Kuei! Ha! ha! ha! ha! ha! *(He bows again.)* This is the second time I welcome   20
you! When did you return? *(Still no answer. He is angry now.)* Well, I have been trying my best to be friendly and have greeted you twice. But you are a man who must be greeted in another way. *(He rolls up his sleeves.)* Look here! Protect yourself!

PRECIOUS STREAM *(coming forward in front of him):*   Stop, you   25
tiger! As you failed to murder him by your plans during the Western Expedition, do you now dare to try to kill him by force? Here you have his wife to deal with! I dare you to try to kill him, you murderer!

SILVER STREAM *(coming to her husband's rescue):*   How can   30
he kill your husband with just one blow?

PRECIOUS STREAM: You won't feel hurt if it is not your husband who receives the blow.

SILVER STREAM: You are most troublesome!

PRECIOUS STREAM: You are the one who is troublesome!   35

GOLDEN STREAM: Please, don't!

(They struggle and Hsieh separates them.)

HSIEH: Sit down, both of you!

WEI: Hsieh Ping-Kuei is very rude. He actually tried to touch my wife! *(He turns to Wang.)* I beg to report to Your Excellency that it really is Hsieh Ping-Kuei who has come back.

5   WANG *(aside):*   He has chosen a very bad time to come!

SU *(after whispering with his wife):*   Will you excuse me, dear Father-in-law and Mother-in-law?

WANG AND MADAM: Certainly.

WEI: Hey, old Su, where are you going?

10   SU: I have some important business at home.

WEI: That's not true. You are trying to get away because you see that something very serious is going to happen between us. Isn't that so?

SU AND GOLDEN STREAM: No, no!

15   WEI: I don't care whether you go or not. I can deal with the matter alone.

SU: Thank you! Good-bye and good luck!

GOLDEN STREAM: Good-bye!

(Su leaves with his wife.)

20   WANG *(rising and coming forward):*   I must welcome him for the sake of my daughter. *(Bowing to Hsieh.)* Welcome, my son-in-law! *(No answer.)* He is rather impolite to me. But I will not think badly of him. Madam, our son-in-law has returned. It is indeed good news!

25   MADAM *(coming forward):*   At last he has come back. *(To Hsieh.)* Why didn't you come earlier, my dear son-in-law?

HSIEH *(kneeling down before her):*   My respects and thanks to you, dear Mother-in-law.

MADAM: Don't stand on ceremony. We have wept very much

30   for you. You must never go away again. How happy I am to see you once more.

HSIEH: Thank you, dear Mother-in-law.

(He takes his seat again.)

PRECIOUS STREAM: You are still as foolish as you used to be!

35   Why do you sit here? Why don't you go and settle your account with Wei, the Tiger?

HSIEH: Don't be in a hurry; everything will be settled soon.

WEI: I don't understand what you are talking about.

WANG *(trying to keep them quiet)*:   Even if we have been a little hard on you, dear son-in-law, remember our position doesn't
allow us to behave otherwise. And you can't complain of the
General's action as long as you are only a captain under him.   5

HSIEH: No! I only want to know why he didn't pay my wife
what was due to me.

WEI: Not another word about your pay! If you prefer to be
unfriendly with me, let me tell you that I could charge you with
running away in time of war and coming back for pay in time of   10
peace! The punishment is death!

SILVER STREAM: Yes, death!

MADAM *(worried)*:   Oh, no! You wouldn't do that, would
you?

WEI: That depends.   15

SILVER STREAM: That depends.

A VOICE *(off stage)*:   Prepare yourselves to receive the Imperial Edict* from His Majesty the Emperor of China!

(All rise and line up.)

A MESSENGER *(coming with a yellow roll in his hands)*:   The   20
Imperial Edict from His Majesty the Emperor of China! *(They
all kneel down. The roll is opened. It contains the two words 'Imperial Edict'. The messenger shows it to the audience and not to
the players, and says aloud.)* 'His Imperial Majesty orders the
Prime Minister, Wang, to welcome His Majesty, Hsieh Ping-   25
Kuei, the King of the Western Regions, to his Court tomorrow,
and bring Wei, the Tiger General, with him, under arrest!' Long
live the Emperor!

ALL *(getting up)*:   We hear and we obey! Long live the
Emperor!   30

(The messenger departs.)

WEI *(kneeling before Hsieh)*:   I beg for your pardon, Your
Majesty!

(Hsieh laughs and turns away.)

PRECIOUS STREAM *(in a voice like Wei's)*:   That depends.   35
(And in a voice like Silver Stream's.) That depends.

Imperial Edict,   an order sent out by a King or an Emperor.

(They all laugh and leave.)

WANG: Good heavens! What shall I do? What shall I do?
(He leaves, his Attendants walking in front of him.)

MADAM *(following her husband, with the Maids)*:   You always
know what to do!

WEI *(miserably)*:   I am a dead man! I am a dead man!
(He leaves without looking at his wife.)

SILVER STREAM *(finding herself alone)*:   I am indeed as good
as a widow already.

(She leaves.)

*We have now the honour of being present at the Court of His
Majesty the King of the Western Regions during his visit to China.
The audience has to suppose that there are rich silk hangings and
soft carpets on the floor, and that the furniture is all of fine wood
though what they see is still the same stage.*

*(Four Attendants come forward and then His Majesty appears
in his royal robes and crown of gold.)*

HSIEH: I left here no more than a beggar and have returned
as a king! *(He sits on the chair.)* As I came here from the Imperial Palace all the streets were filled with people who kept throwing flowers at me. If they had shown even the slightest interest
in me eighteen years ago, when I was performing my best acts
of strength in those very streets, they would have made me a
much happier man than they do now! Now I do not care
much about their cheers. My only happiness is the company of
my Queen ! *(He calls.)* Attendants!

ATTENDANTS: Yes, Your Majesty!

HSIEH: Request Her Majesty the Queen to come to Court.

ATTENDANTS: Yes, Your Majesty!

*(One of the Attendants goes to the right entrance and calls loud-
ly)*:   His Majesty requests the presence of Her Majesty the
Queen!

A VOICE *(off stage)*:   To hear is to obey.

*(Following two Maidservants, Precious Stream appears in her
queenly robes, which make her lovelier than ever.)*

PRECIOUS STREAM: After wearing rags for eighteen years, I
now have the joy of being in royal robes. *(She turns and curtsies*

to Hsieh.) Your humble wife presents her respects to Your Majesty!

HSIEH *(happily)*:   Thank you. Don't stand on ceremony, but please be seated.

PRECIOUS STREAM: Thank you. *(She is helped to sit at his   5 side.)* May I ask Your Majesty what happened when you were received at the Emperor's Court?

HSIEH: It was a great success. The Emperor has ordered the prisoner Wei to be sent here.

PRECIOUS STREAM: Excellent! What has Your Majesty done   10 with him?

HSIEH: Nothing yet. I want you to decide for me.

PRECIOUS STREAM: Very good. Have him brought here.

HSIEH: Attendants!

ATTENDANTS: Yes, Your Majesty!   15

HSIEH: Order them to bring the prisoner Wei here.

ATTENDANTS: Yes, Your Majesty!

(One of the Attendants goes to the right and calls):   Bring the prisoner Wei here at once.

A VOICE *(off stage)*:   Without delay.   20

(Wei, with his hands tied behind his back, appears without gown and hat. He has a guard on either side of him, and an Executioner* with a big knife behind him.)

WEI: When I heard that I was wanted here I almost fainted. *(He kneels before Hsieh.)* The prisoner Wei awaits Your Majes-   25 ty's pleasure!

HSIEH: Who is kneeling before me?

WEI: The prisoner, Wei.

HSIEH: Do you admit that you planned to kill me during the Western Expedition?   30

WEI *(hanging down his head)*:   I admit it. I only beg for your pardon, Your Majesty!

PRECIOUS STREAM: Do you admit that you have been cheating me of what was due to me in order to make me die of hunger?

WEI: I admit it. I only beg for your pardon, my dear sister—   35 eh—Your Majesty!

**Executioner,*   a person appointed by the law to kill people.

PRECIOUS STREAM: How can you be pardoned? Don't you remember that only a short time ago you said you would never be
under my control? What have you to say now?

WEI: I was blind then.

5   PRECIOUS STREAM: You didn't think you were blind then.
And don't you remember that you also said you wouldn't care
even if you were under my control?

WEI: I was mad then.

PRECIOUS STREAM: You seemed to be anything but mad then.

10   No, you will not be pardoned.

HSIEH: No, you will not be pardoned. Therefore the punishment for your crime...

PRECIOUS STREAM *(correcting him)*:   For your many crimes.

HSIEH: Yes, the punishment for your many crimes is... *(look-*

15   *ing at his wife, who crosses her throat with her arm)* is death!

WEI: Oh, no!

HSIEH: Executioner!

EXECUTIONER *(kneeling)*:   Yes, Your Majesty!

HSIEH: Kill the prisoner!

20   EXECUTIONER: Yes, Your Majesty!

(Wei rises, and the two guards lead him to a corner to be killed.)

A VOICE *(off stage)*:   Please, Executioner, wait a moment!

(They stop. Silver Stream rushes forward.)

SILVER STREAM: Oh, I am so glad to have come in time! I will

25   ask my brother-in-law for his pardon! I have heard people say
that many lives have been saved by wives arriving just in time.

WEI: Please don't waste your time in talking to the audience
but go in and ask for pardon at once!

SILVER STREAM: You terrible man! You deserve death! *(She*

30   *turns and kneels before Hsieh.)* My respects to Your Majesty, my
dear brother-in-law!

HSIEH: Who is kneeling before me?

SILVER STREAM: Your Majesty's sister-in-law, Silver Stream.

HSIEH: What have you come here for?

35   SILVER STREAM: To ask for my husband's pardon.

HSIEH *(looking at his wife, who shakes her head)*:   No! You
have both behaved very badly to us. I cannot pardon him.

SILVER STREAM *(getting up and going out)* :   Nothing can be done now.

WEI :   You have come in time only to see me die!

SILVER STREAM *(departing)* :   Let me call for help!

EXECUTIONER :   Let me finish my job. The sooner the better.   *5*
(He raises his knife.)

A VOICE *(off stage)* :   Executioner, pray wait a minute! *(He stops. Silver Stream appears again dragging her father forward by his arm.)*

SILVER STREAM :   Quick, Father! *(Calling out aloud.)* His Ex-   *10*
cellency the Prime Minister, Wang, is here!

FIRST ATTENDANT *(kneeling)* :   I beg to report to Your Majesty that His Excellency the Prime Minister, Wang, is coming.

HSIEH *(looking at his wife, who shakes her head)* :   Tell His Excellency that I can't see him at present, but if he will wait a few   *15*
hours I may give him a few seconds then.

WANG *(angrily)* : Oh! My God! *(He faints.)*

EXECUTIONER *(raising his knife)* :   Now for it!

A VOICE *(off stage)* :   Executioner, do wait a second! *(He stops. Silver Stream appears, dragging Su and Golden Stream   *20*
forward.)*

SILVER STREAM :   Oh, quick! It's a matter of life and death!
(Calling out aloud.) His Honour, General Su, and his wife are coming.

FIRST ATTENDANT *(kneeling)* :   I beg to report to Your Majes-   *25*
ty that His Honour, General Su, and his wife are coming!

HSIEH *(looking at his wife)* :   Tell His Honour, General Su, and his wife that I shall be very glad to receive them if they promise not to refer in any way to the prisoner who is to die.

FIRST ATTENDANT :   Yes, Your Majesty.   *30*

SILVER STREAM :   Heaven have mercy on me! I have been running to and fro in vain! There is still one more chance. *(She departs for the third time.)*

FIRST ATTENDANT *(going to Su and Golden Stream)* :   His Majesty says he will be very glad to receive you if you mention   *35*
nothing about the prisoner who is to die.

SU AND GOLDEN STREAM :   That's very hard! We have come

specially on his account.

EXECUTIONER: I am sorry. I can't wait any longer! *(He raises his knife.)*

A VOICE *(off stage)*:   Executioner, do wait a little!

(The Executioner puts down his knife and is obviously very annoyed at the delay. Silver Stream appears for the last time, dragging Madam along with her.)

SILVER STREAM: Quick, Mother, you are my last hope! *(Calling out loud.)* Madam is coming!

FIRST ATTENDANT *(kneeling)*:   I beg to report to Your Majesty that Madam your mother-in-law is coming.!

HSIEH *(to the Attendant)*:   All right! *(Rising.)* We must go to welcome her.

PRECIOUS STREAM *(rising also)*:   Yes, let us go at once!

(They go to greet Madam.)

HSIEH *(holding his hands together and bowing very low)*:   My respects to you, my dear mother-in-law.

PRECIOUS STREAM *(curtsying)*:   My respects, dear Mother.

MADAM: Don't stand on ceremony, dear children. *(Seeing her husband.)* What are you standing here for, dear?

WANG: I was told to wait here for a few hours before he could give me a few seconds!

MADAM: Ha! ha! You deserve it! *(Seeing her eldest daughter and Su.)* And what are you here for, my children?

SU: We came to ask them to pardon Wei.

GOLDEN STREAM: But His Majesty forbade us to mention anything about the prisoner.

MADAM: Oh, so that's it! *(She taps her fingers on her forehead.)* Of course, we mustn't mention the prisoner to His Majesty.

SILVER STREAM *(worried)*:   But you...

MADAM: Foolish child! Come with me, all of you, and let me have His Majesty's word of honour that he will not mention even the name of Wei to me!

HSIEH: I gladly give you my word!

SILVER STREAM *(who can't be silent now)*:   And you said you would not mention my husband to His Majesty?

MADAM: Certainly! I give him my word of honour, too. *(To Hsieh.)* Isn't that fair?

SILVER STREAM: Oh, Mother! How can you?

MADAM *(planning something)*:   Silence! Don't let me hear you speak again!

(Everybody is asked to take a seat.)

PRECIOUS STREAM *(pleased)*:   Mother, you are very under-standing!

MADAM: Am I? I want to ask a favour of you and I hope you will show how understanding you are.

PRECIOUS STREAM: Of course I will. What is it, dear Mother? Before you say the word, you may have your wish.

MADAM: That's very kind of you. *(She rises and curtsies to her daughter, who returns the curtsy uneasily.)* I must thank Your Majesty properly!

PRECIOUS STREAM: Please do not, dear Mother! What is it?

MADAM: I want you to pardon Wei!

(Everyone is surprised.)

PRECIOUS STREAM: But you have given your word of honour that you would never mention him!

MADAM: Yes, to His Majesty! Not to *Her* Majesty!

HSIEH: But he deserves more than death!

MADAM: No! Remember your promise and don't mention him to me, Your Majesty!

HSIEH *(seeing that he has fallen into her trap)*:   Well, I'm caught!

MADAM: Since Her Majesty has granted my request...

PRECIOUS STREAM: No, I have not!

MADAM: Yes, you have! You told me that I could have what I wished, even before I said a word! And I thanked you for your favour.

PRECIOUS STREAM: I thought you would never say a word for him.

MADAM: I am only asking a favour and I am not going to say a word to defend him.

PRECIOUS STREAM: Well, even if I have promised you I am afraid my husband won't listen to me.

HSIEH *(seeing a way out):*   No, I won't.

MADAM: But you must. All the best families of this and every other land are ruled by the wife. My husband here will tell you that he has always listened to me, and he will always have to
5 listen to me! He will set a good example for you! *(To her husband.)* Don't you, my dear?

WANG *(unwillingly):*   Eh—eh—I do.

MADAM: And willingly!

WANG: Eh—eh—yes—willingly.

10 PRECIOUS STREAM: Dear Mother, you are indeed a darling. *(To her husband.)* As I already promised my mother I am afraid you will have to carry out my promise.

HSIEH: I said it was for you to decide.

MADAM: Excellent!

15 ALL: Excellent!

PRECIOUS STREAM: His life may be spared, but he must be punished in some other way. I think a few strokes on his back might meet the case.

SILVER STREAM: Yes, I, too, think that he ought to be beaten,
20 for he has behaved badly to me.

PRECIOUS STREAM: Yes, he really deserves to be beaten severely.

WEI *(shouting):*   Oh, no! I'd rather die! I'd rather die!

(They all laugh.)

25 HSIEH: Attendants!

ATTENDANTS: Yes, Your Majesty!

HSIEH: Bring the prisoner here to be beaten.

ATTENDANTS: Yes, Your Majesty!

(One of the Attendants moves forward and says to the Guards):
30 His Majesty orders the prisoner to be brought before him!

GUARDS: Yes!

(The Executioner goes out.)

(Wei is brought to the Court and kneels down again.)

MADAM: Now thank Their Majesties for their kindness!

35 WEI: Must I thank them when they wish to have me beaten?

MADAM: You must!

WEI: Good heavens! *(To Hsieh and Precious Stream.)* I

thank Your Majesties for your great kindness.

HSIEH *(To Guards):*   Beat him. *(Looking at his wife, who holds up four fingers.)* Give him four hundred strokes on the back!

GUARDS: Yes, Your Majesty!

(They prepare by putting one of their bamboo poles on Wei's   5
back whilst the other pole is used to beat the pole on his back.)

WEI: I shall be a dead man long before they finish!

PRECIOUS STREAM *(stopping them):*   Stop! Forty strokes will be enough.

HSIEH *(telling them to strike):*   All right. Forty strokes.   10

GUARDS: Yes, Your Majesty! *(They count the strokes aloud by fives and Wei yells 'Ouch!' after each blow.)* Five *('Ouch!'),* Ten *('Ouch!'),* Fifteen *('Ouch!'),* Twenty *('Ouch!'),* Twenty-five *('Ouch!'),* Thirty *('Ouch!'),* Thirty-five *('Ouch!'),* Forty *('Ouch!').* We have given forty strokes, Your Majesty!

HSIEH: You may leave him here.

GUARDS: Yes, Your Majesty! *(They leave.)*

PRECIOUS STREAM: Now, let us forgive and forget what has happened in the past. *(To Wei.)* Take a seat beside your wife.

5 SILVER STREAM: You must thank Their Majesties.

WEI *(getting up with difficulty)*: Oh, thank you, indeed! *(He tries to sit down.)* Ouch! Ouch! *(He stands with his arms leaning on the back of a chair.)*

SILVER STREAM: Why don't you sit down? Why do you stand
10 in such a position?

WEI *(very sorry for himself)*: How can I sit down with wounds like mine?

SILVER STREAM *(smiling)*: This will keep you from being wicked for a long time!

15 MADAM *(smiling)*: Yes, it will! *(To Wang.)* Don't be angry, dear! Aren't you glad to see all our children happily united?

WANG: I am.

PRECIOUS STREAM: Oh, dear Mother, there is someone who has lately joined our family. You mustn't go before meeting her.

20 ALL *(surprised)*: Who is she!

PRECIOUS STREAM: My sister-in-law! *(To Hsieh.)* Isn't she your sister, dear?

HSIEH *(uncomfortably)*: Ah—eh—yes!

MADAM: But we never knew that you had a sister!

25 PRECIOUS STREAM: Neither did he, until recently. I haven't even seen her yet.

GOLDEN STREAM: Where is she?

PRECIOUS STREAM: I know that she is waiting here.

SILVER STREAM: Ask her to come at once, please.

30 PRECIOUS STREAM: Yes, please.

HSIEH: Attendants!

ATTENDANTS: Yes, Your Majesty!

HSIEH: Request Her Highness, my sister, to come here.

ATTENDANTS: Yes, Your Majesty!

35 *(One of the Attendants goes to the right entrance and calls loudly)*: His Majesty requests the presence of Her Highness, his sister.

A VOICE *(off stage)*:   To hear is to obey.

(The Princess appears with her two officers, Ma Ta and Kiang Hai. They have never seen such wonderful surroundings before and are looking at the ceiling, the walls, the carpets, and the furniture with wide open eyes.)

MA TA: I beg to report to Your Highness that this is the Court of His Majesty.

PRINCESS: Indeed! *(She looks round.)* What a strange place it is! *(To audience.)* China is indeed a strange land. Everything is just the opposite of what is in our country.

KIANG HAI: Yes. For example we always wear woollen clothes, but they always wear silk.

PRINCESS: Never mind about that. After they have seen some of us in our own land I am sure they will order some woollen stuff from the Western Regions. The only difficult thing is their many ceremonies. To one who has been in the Western Regions and is used to the freedom there, their strange customs are most troublesome. *(She turns and looks at Hsieh carefully.)* Ma Ta and Kiang Hai!

MA AND KIANG: Yes, Your Highness!

PRINCESS: Who is the man sitting there like the King of Heaven?

MA TA: That is His Majesty, our King!

PRINCESS: How changed he is! I am a little afraid of him. *(She turns and stands very far from Hsieh.)* My respects to Your Majesty! *(She greets him.)*

HSIEH: I am very glad to see you. Please don't stand on ceremony.

PRINCESS: Thank you! *(To Ma and Kiang.)* Ma Ta! Kiang Hai!

MA AND KIANG: Yes, Your Highness!

PRINCESS: Who is that little goddess sitting next to His Majesty?

KIANG HAI: That is his wife, the famous Precious Stream of the Wang family. Why do you call her a goddess?

PRINCESS: Don't you see that even her eyelids do not move at all?

KIANG HAI: That is the custom in China. They are not allowed to move even their eyelids before strangers.

PRINCESS: Oh, I can't stand this! Let us go back to the
Western Regions.

5   MA AND KIANG: Oh, no, we can't!

PRINCESS: What am I to do?

MA TA: You must go to her and greet her.

PRINCESS: I won't greet her.

KIANG HAI: If you don't they will say that women of the
10   Western Regions have very bad manners!

PRINCESS: Then I must do it for the reputation of our women.

MA AND KIANG: Yes, Your Highness!

PRINCESS *(going nearer to Precious Stream)*:   My respects to
you, the famous Precious Stream of the Wang family! *(She greets
15   her by putting her hand to her forehead. As Precious Stream has
never received a soldier's greeting like this before she raises both
her hands in fright.)* Ma Ta! Kiang Hai!

MA AND KIANG: Yes, Your Highness!

PRINCESS: Why does she appear to try to fly when I greet her?
20   MA TA: She isn't trying to fly. She is returning your greeting.

PRINCESS: That is not a greeting.

KIANG HAI: She has never done this before. Their way of
greeting is quite different from ours.

PRINCESS: What is the difference?
25   MA TA: Our way of greeting is like raising the hand to hit a
dog. *(He does so.)*

KIANG HAI: Their way is like stirring cream. *(He does so.)*

PRINCESS *(trying to 'stir cream' also)*:   How stupid!

MA TA: They say that the 'hitting a dog' greeting is equally,
30   if not more, stupid!

PRINCESS: Well, I must try to 'stir cream' in her honour.

MA AND KIANG: Yes, Your Highness!

PRINCESS: Watch me, Ma Ta and Kiang Hai. *(She goes up
again, holds her hands together and stirs the imaginary cream
35   rapidly.)* My respects to you!

PRECIOUS STREAM *(smiling and rising to curtsy to her)*:   Many
thanks! Please don't stand on ceremony. *(Aside.)* How charming

the Princess is! Now I can understand why my husband didn't return to me earlier! He was undoubtedly attracted by her beauty for those eighteen years. If I were a man I should like to stay in the Western Regions for a few years too! As I am a woman, I hate her. I do not wish to speak with her, but if I do not she will say that   *5*
the women of China are very impolite. For the reputation of the women in China I must say a few kind words to her. *(To the Princess.)* I thank you for having entertained my husband for me all these eighteen years!

PRINCESS *(aside)*:   Ah, she is joking! *(To Precious Stream.)*   *10*
Oh, you needn't be; I was only too happy to do so!

PRECIOUS STREAM *(angry, aside)*:   The little devil! *(To the Princess.)* This is my father, and this is my mother. *(They rise and the Princess 'stirs cream' again.)* And these are my sisters and brothers-in-law.   *15*

PRINCESS *('stirring cream' once more)*:   But this man seems to have no face! *(She touches Wei's back.)*

WEI: Ouch! Ouch! *(Turning round and showing his beautiful face to her.)*

PRINCESS *(frightened)*:   Oh! Oh! I must go. I must go.   *20*

PRECIOUS STREAM: Wait a moment, please! *(She whispers to Hsieh.)* So-and-so, So-and-so!

HSIEH: Yes! Yes! *(He calls.)* Attendants!

ATTENDANTS: Yes, Your Majesty!

HSIEH: Request So-and-so to come to court immediately.   *25*

ATTENDANTS: Yes, Your Majesty!

ATTENDANT *(going to the right entrance and calling loudly)*:
His Majesty requests the presence of So-and-so immediately.

A VOICE *(off stage)*:   Coming!

(His Excellency the Minister of Foreign Affairs is a man of the   *30*
world who must have travelled in many foreign countries. He walks quickly forward.)

MINISTER: Your most obedient humble servant, So-and-so, the Minister of Foreign Affairs. *(He bows gracefully to Hsieh.)*
My respects to Your Majesty!   *35*

HSIEH: Thank you! Don't stand on ceremony. I want to tell you that my sister, the Princess of the Western Regions, has

arrived here today. I hope you will welcome her and see that
she has everything that she wants.

    MINISTER: Yes, Your Majesty! Delighted, Your Majesty!
(He turns to the Princess and kisses her hand.) My sincerest wel-
5   come and respects to Your Highness!

    PRINCESS *(who seems to like him):*   Oh, thank you!

    MINISTER *(offering his arm):*   Will Your Highness come with
me?

    PRINCESS: With pleasure. *(She takes his arm and looks at
10   him lovingly.)*

MINISTER: Excuse me, Your Majesty! Good morning, every-body!

PRINCESS: Good-bye, everybody! Tell me, where did you learn such nice manners, Your Excellency?

(They leave looking at each other.) 5

WANG: Disgusting! *(Getting up.)* Excuse me. I must go back!

MADAM: Shocking! *(Joining him.)* Good-bye, my children!
(They leave.)

SU AND GOLDEN STREAM: It is disgusting! *(Rising.)* Good-bye. We must go back. 10

(They leave.)

WEI AND SILVER STREAM: It is a shame! *(Rising.)* Good-bye and thank you!

(They leave.)

5   HSIEH: Let us leave too. *(He rises and the Attendants leave first.)*

PRECIOUS STREAM *(coming to Hsieh):* Do you always behave as those two were doing in the Western Regions? Why not show me?

10   HSIEH: For shame! Our friendship is for each other, and not for public entertainment!

(He leaves.)

PRECIOUS STREAM *(copying the way they had spoken and the actions of the Minister and Princess):* 'My sincerest welcome
15 and respects to Your Highness!' *(She kisses her own hand.)* 'Oh, thank you!' *(She offers her arm.)* 'Will Your Highness come with me?' *(She takes the offered arm.)* 'With pleasure!'

(She leaves with her imaginary companion.)

— THE END —

Questions

Act I
1. Do you think Prime Minister Wang really loved his third daughter, Precious Stream? Give reasons for your answer.
2. What kind of people are General Wei and Silver Stream?
3. Why do you think Precious Stream chose to marry Hsieh Ping-Kuei?
4. Who were those who objected to Precious Stream's choice of a husband, and why?

Act II
1. What was the reason General Wei gave for not giving Precious Stream the things that were promised?
2. Why did Precious Stream refuse to return to the palace with her mother?
3. How many months or years have passed between the beginning of Act I and the end of Act II?

Act III
1. How did Hsieh Ping-Kuei become King of the Western Regions?
2. Why did Hsieh Ping-Kuei stay in the Western Regions for eighteen years?
3. Why did Hsieh Ping-Kuei test Lady Precious Stream when they met again after eighteen years?
4. When Hsieh Ping-Kuei made Precious Stream his Queen she said, 'At Last.' Why do you think she said this?

Act IV
1. Why did Hsieh Ping-Kuei send his wife to the Prime Minister's house before him?
2. General Wei found it difficult to believe that Hsieh Ping-Kuei had come back. What was the reason?
3. Do you think Wei deserved the punishment he received? Why?
4. Precious Stream obviously did not believe that the Princess of the Western Regions was Hsieh's sister. What did she say to show this?

NOTE ON LANGUAGE

Certain phrases, which are used as polite expressions in the play, may not be known by the reader. Most of them are not usual in everyday English.

To pay one's respects to someone	to make a very polite visit or to greet someone with respect
At your service Your humble servant	express willingness to do something for someone else
I am much obliged Thank you all the same	thank you
Don't mention it Only too delighted	answer to someone's thanks
Don't stand on ceremony	used as part of the usual form of old Chinese greeting

Some other phrases, which are used in the play, are also not usual in everyday English.

For example: third sister, eldest brother.

OXFORD PROGRESSIVE ENGLISH READERS

GRADE 1

Vocabulary restricted to 1900 head words
Illustrated partly in two and partly in full colours
One illustration every 6 pages on average

The Adventures of Hang Tuah	MUBIN SHEPPARD
Alice's Adventures in Wonderland	LEWIS CARROLL
A Christmas Carol	CHARLES DICKENS
Don Quixote	CERVANTES
Great Expectations	CHARLES DICKENS
Gulliver's Travels	JONATHAN SWIFT
The House of Sixty Fathers	MEINDERT DEJONG
Islands in the Sky	ARTHUR C. CLARKE
Jane Eyre	CHARLOTTE BRONTË
Little Women	LOUISA M. ALCOTT
Madam White Snake	RETOLD BY BENJAMIN CHIA
Oliver Twist	CHARLES DICKENS
Plays for Malaysian Schools I	PATRICK YEOH
The Stone Junk	RETOLD BY D.H. HOWE
Stories of Shakespeare's Plays I	RETOLD BY N. KATES
The Tale of the Bounty	RETOLD BY H.G. WYATT
Tales from Tolstoy	RETOLD BY R.D. BINFIELD
Tales of Si Kabayan	MURTAGH MURPHY
The Talking Tree & Other Stories	DAVID McROBBIE
The Tiger of Lembah Pahit	NORMA R. YOUNGBERG
A Time of Darkness	SHAMUS FRAZER
The Adventures of Tom Sawyer	MARK TWAIN
Treasure Island	R.L. STEVENSON

GRADE 2

Vocabulary restricted to 2900 head words
One two-coloured illustration every 10 pages on average

Around the World in Eighty Days	JULES VERNE
Asia Pacific Stories	MURTAGH MURPHY
Beau Geste	P.C. WREN
Chinese Tales of the Supernatural	RETOLD BY BENJAMIN CHIA
The Crocodile Dies Twice	SHAMUS FRAZER
David Copperfield	CHARLES DICKENS
Five Tales	OSCAR WILDE
The Hound of the Baskervilles	SIR ARTHUR CONAN DOYLE
The Missing Scientist	S.F. STEVENS
Plays for Malaysian Schools II	PATRICK YEOH
Robinson Crusoe	DANIEL DEFOE
Seven Chinese Stories	T.J. SHERIDAN
Stories of Shakespeare's Plays II	RETOLD BY WYATT & FULLERTON
A Tale of Two Cities	CHARLES DICKENS
Tales of Crime & Detection	RETOLD BY G.F. WEAR
Two Famous English Comedies	RETOLD BY RICHARD CROFT
Vanity Fair	W.M. THACKERAY

GRADE 3
Vocabulary restricted to 3500 head words
One two-coloured illustration every 15 pages on average

Animal Farm	GEORGE ORWELL
The Gifts & Other Stories	O. HENRY & OTHERS
Journey to the Centre of the Earth	JULES VERNE
Kidnapped	R.L. STEVENSON
King Solomon's Mines	H. RIDER HAGGARD
Lady Precious Stream	S.I. HSIUNG
The Moonstone	WILKIE COLLINS
A Night of Terror & Other Strange Tales	GUY DE MAUPASSANT
Pride and Prejudice	JANE AUSTEN
The Red Winds	SHAMUS FRAZER
Seven Stories	H.G. WELLS
Stories of Shakespeare's Plays III	RETOLD BY H.G. WYATT
Tales of Mystery & Imagination	EDGAR ALLAN POE
The War of the Worlds	H.G. WELLS
20,000 Leagues under the Sea	JULES VERNE
Wuthering Heights	EMILY BRONTË